SUCCESS WITH
MEDITERRANEAN
GARDENS

SUCCESS WITH
MEDITERRANEAN
GARDENS

Shirley-Anne Bell

GUILD OF MASTER CRAFTSMAN
PUBLICATIONS LTD

First published 2005 by
Guild of Master Craftsman Publications Ltd,
Castle Place, 166 High Street, Lewes,
East Sussex, BN7 1XU

Illustrations by John Yates

ISBN 1 86108 450 1

A catalogue record of this book is available from the British Library.

Production Manager: Hilary MacCallum
Managing Editor: Gerrie Purcell
Project Editor: Dominique Page

Designed by Andy Harrison
Set in Futura

Colour origination by Masterpiece, London
Printed and bound in Singapore by Kyodo Printing Co. Ltd.

Acknowledgements

Special thanks to my editor Dominique Page for all her hard work and patience, to designer Andy Harrison for making the book so visually exciting and to illustrator John Yates for making sense of my plans and drawings.

And thanks, of course, to my husband Neville who has done the lion's share of the photography and for all the travelling and talks we have done together to research the material for the book.

Thank you also to all the members of garden societies and other clubs in the East Midlands, England, where we have picked your brains shamelessly for definitions of Mediterranean-style gardening during the talks we have given.

Grateful acknowledgements are due to all the people who have allowed Neville and I to use photographs of their gardens, particularly to the owners of the following gardens open to the public (please see appendix for more details): Ayscoughfee Hall and Gardens, Lincolnshire; Valerie and Simon Lister, Bicton Park Botanical Gardens, Devon; Capel Manor College, Middlesex; Cotswold Wildlife Park and Gardens, Oxfordshire and head gardener Tim Miles; East Ruston Old Vicarage Garden, Norfolk; Eden Project, Cornwall; Earl and Countess of Sandwich, Mapperton Gardens, Dorset; Newstead Abbey Park, Nottinghamshire; Pine Lodge Garden and Nursery, Cornwall; Probus Gardens, Cornwall; National Trust Overbecks Museum and Garden, Devon and particular thanks to head gardener Nick Stewart for all his help; Lord Reresby Sitwell, Renishaw Hall, Sheffield; Royal Horticultural Society, RHS Rosemoor, Devon; Tresco Abbey Gardens, Isles of Scilly. And also to the owners of Lincolnshire gardens including Mr and Mrs Brown, Mr and Mrs N Patterson, Mr and Mrs I Roberts, the family of the late Jean Smith and Swineshead Primary School, and thanks also to Mr P Freeland of Sussex for showing us his unique cliff cactus garden, Mrs L Heppleston of Scarborough for letting us photograph her mosaics, and to Kate Elysee of Kate Elysee Garden Design, Poole, Dorset (+44 (0)1202 876284) for sharing her designs so generously, and to her clients for allowing us to see their gardens. Thanks also to Natural Driftwood Sculptures (www.driftwoodsculptures.co.uk, Tel: +44 (0)1202 578274) for allowing me to feature some of their pieces.

Contents

LEFT **Abbey Garden, Tresco, Isles of Scilly, south-west England**

Introduction

Besides running our nursery, my husband Neville and I give regular talks to garden clubs and women's institutes. One of our most popular is called 'Mediterranean-style Gardening in Temperate Gardens'. Often we will ask the audience to discuss what comes to mind when they think of the Mediterranean and its gardens. Colour and brilliant light, sun, sand and sea, good food and wine are always mentioned. But physical things also materialize, things that can be transferred to cooler climates while still encapsulating that ambience, such as courtyards and terraces, terracotta roof tiles, colour-washed walls, mosaics, statues, plants in containers, water features, especially formal pools and fountains, pencil-thin cypresses, formal and geometrical garden layouts with box parterres, climbing plants like vines, ivy, hibiscus and bougainvillea, and last, but not least, unfamiliar plants with dazzling colours and exotic flowers.

As you can see from this fairly extensive list, Mediterranean-style gardening is a loose definition and there is scope for a variety of styles; there is therefore bound to be something that will suit your personality and lifestyle. This book aims to cover them all with a wide range of design ideas, illustrated with lots of examples of inspirational, thriving gardens in temperate climates.

You can choose from formal gardens, like the clean and minimalist, with modern materials and sparse but dramatic planting, or the more classical, with topiary and geometrical patterns of paths and hedges. You can create an Islamic-inspired water or courtyard garden, have an alternative herbaceous border with exotic planting or an abundant Mediterranean-style meadow with ornamental grasses and loads of flowers. Alternatively, you can go for a lush, romantic look with scented plants, climbers, scrambling ivies and an altogether more exuberant feel, or go out on a limb with a subtropical look or an exotic mini desert. Whatever your preference, you will find the inspiration and guidance for creating your own Mediterranean-style garden within this book.

LEFT **Inspirational planting in the contemporary Mediterranean Garden, Bicton Park Gardens, Devon, south-west England**

SECTION 1

LEFT **Mapperton Gardens,
Dorset, south-west England**

CHAPTER 1

What is Mediterranean gardening?

Before you can begin to plan your Mediterranean-style garden you need to have a picture of the real thing – the Mediterranean and Mediterranean-climate gardens that are the archetypal style of garden you would like to create.

You need to bear in mind that these gardens have developed in areas that have hot, almost completely dry, summers and sunny, though wet, winters, with the lowest temperature falling within the range of 35°F (2°C) to 21°F (–6°C). Therefore, the threat to plants is from drought, not the colder, damper climate of temperate gardens.

THE CHARACTERISTICS

The gardens are characterized by an absence of lawns and herbaceous borders and a prevalence of hard landscaping, with walls, steps, paths, terraces and statues. There is

ABOVE **The Hanbury Gardens in La Mortola, northern Italy, flow down a series of terraces to the Mediterranean sea below**

ABOVE **This windowsill in Biot, in the south of France, is crammed with containers housing easy-care, drought-resistant plants**

ABOVE **Massed pelargoniums, like these in Spain, can turn the smallest space into a riot of colour all summer long**

ABOVE **The gardens of the Generalife, Alhambra Palace, Spain, show the Moorish style, with geometrical water features**

wide use of containers, not for half-hardy planting in the summer, but because it makes best use of scarce and expensive water. The soil is often poor or the terrain steep, and land costs are high, so plots tend to be small.

There is a great importance placed on the development of areas of shade and privacy. The gardens, therefore, feature patios, terraces

ABOVE *Zantedeschia aethiopica* in the Spanish garden, Villa Ephrussi de Rothschild, near Nice in the south of France

LEFT This photograph of Mapperton Gardens in Dorset, south-west England, shows how the basic elements of the Italian-style Mediterranean garden – clipped evergreens and hard landscaping – can be transferred to a temperate climate, where they will withstand all weather conditions

and pergolas. This use of hard landscaping, terracing, steps and containers gives a formality and geometry which is reminiscent of the gardens of the Romans, recreated across Europe under the influence of the Italian Renaissance. This is also epitomized by the Moorish- and Italian-influenced courtyards, enclosed by hedging, topiary or walls and containing a shady, private garden, often with a water feature that acts as a refuge from the heat.

Evergreens – often severely clipped into hedges and topiary – add to the sense of formality, which is nevertheless softened with an extravagance of

ABOVE **Citrus groves, like this one at The Hanbury Gardens, La Mortola, northern Italy, are the embodiment of the Mediterranean garden**

planting spilling out of tubs and containers, rampaging over walls and alongside steps, and hanging in trusses from pergolas and arbours.

Planting schemes are often diverse. The nineteenth century was a great period of discovery for plant hunters, and their new introductions were coveted and acquired by gardeners all over Europe, who displayed them as prizes in their gardens. Many of these plant introductions, including palms, cacti and the other succulents, have become naturalized in the Mediterranean. There is also an interest in terms of utility and convenience in the use of drought-proof plants in steep hillside and cliffside gardens, and to provide luxuriant curtains of foliage to soften walls and steps.

Other evocative plants include olive, citrus, and *Nerium oleander*. Lavish, colourful climbers include jasmines, bougainvillea and plumbago.

ABOVE **These fields of aromatic lavender, stretching as far as the eye can see, are grown for the perfume industry**

There are grey-leaved plants, such as santolina, achillea and verbascum. Aromatic plants like jasmine, acacia and citrus, and the culinary and medicinal herbs, including lavender, thyme, angelica, fennel, rosemary and sage, are there in abundance. And there are the bulbs and rhizomes like agapanthus, crocosmia and cannas, plus colourful flowering plants including pelargoniums, cistus, helianthemum and kniphofia.

15

There is also an increasing interest in growing and conserving native species in Mediterranean-climate areas. The wildflower meadows of the Mediterranean and Mediterranean-climate regions are filled with a spring flush of flowers, as the plants need to grow, flower and seed before the dry summer season sets in. In temperate areas with higher summer rainfall these species delight us with flowers all summer long, instead of with the brief displays they present in their natural habitat.

The natural habitats include the Mediterranean maquis, the Californian chapparal and the South African fynbos, which have given us our summer annuals and more tender perennials, like the

LEFT **The Mediterranean native habit is known as the maquis and it supports tough native species including cistus or rock roses with their ephemeral flowers along with aromatic herbs like lavender, thyme and rosemary**

BELOW **Californian wild flower meadow or chapparal in the Warm Temperate Biome at the Eden Project, Cornwall, south-east England**

santolinas, eschscholzias, osteospermums and arctotis. In the lands that border the Mediterranean, the maquis supports evergreen shrubby vegetation, including *Chamaerops humilis* 'the European fan palm', *Olea europaea* 'the wild olive', strawberry and bay trees, species of cistus or rock roses and rosemary. Poorer soils and heavily grazed areas support tough, low-growing and sparse vegetation, such as lavenders, thyme, phlomis and euphorbia.

The South African fynbos or 'fine bush' flora has developed in fire- and drought-prone poor soils. Along with the Californian foothills, these areas have provided us a range of showy annuals, including those of the chapparal and the Namaqualand daisies, like osteospermum, felicia and arctotis, as well as glorious shrubs and climbers like ceanothus, the Californian lilac.

In addition, the Chilean matorral, from *mata*, the Spanish for shrub, has given us the wine palm *Jubaea chilensis*, *Araucaria araucana* 'the monkey puzzle tree', alstroemeria and the nasturtium *Tropaeolum majus*.

RIGHT The Botanical Garden in Amsterdam, the Netherlands, runs along the canal side. A strip of ground between the glasshouses and the water's edge has been turned into a meadow blooming with a diverse mass of wild flowers

BELOW The precious habitat of the South African fynbos is one of the richest sources in the world for wild flower species

The Advantages

THEY DO NOT REQUIRE LARGE PLOTS

Space in temperate areas is under pressure, so today's developers have tended to concentrate on the highest-possible density of housing, which means that garden space is often sacrificed, both at the front and the back of houses. This occurs even more when houses have been subdivided into flats and especially with apartment blocks. As a result, modern homes often have small plots.

In Mediterranean areas land is also often at a premium. These are desirable areas to live in or to visit so house prices are high. Furthermore, geographically, space is tight, with steep slopes and terracing, so plots are small. This means that the garden styles transfer very well to small gardens in temperate areas. A Mediterranean-style garden can fit in the tiniest corner, running alongside a drive, garage, path or steps, or on the smallest balcony. Mediterranean-style pergolas and arbours, which are used to give essential shade in relentlessly sunny gardens, are also ideal for giving privacy in plots that can be overlooked on every side.

Even with older housing that often has larger plots, there is such a need for car-parking space that the area for actual gardening is severely limited, and front gardens in particular disappear under a driveway for the family's car or, more commonly, cars. Though, of course, nineteenth- and early twentieth-century terraces often have little more than a flight of steps down to a tiny space that would not even hold a car.

THEY CAN CREATE A 'ROOM' WITHIN LARGER PLOTS

If you are fortunate enough to have a large garden, this style of gardening makes an ideal compartment within a larger site – like a patio area, for example, which has its own identity and therefore needs a certain approach to landscaping and design.

THEY EVOKE RELAXATION

Mediterranean-style gardening fits perfectly with the idea of the garden as an extra room for relaxation and not for yet more work. Though lots of people love gardening and relish the hours that they spend on difficult and time-consuming plants and styles of garden, there are many others that view their garden as a sanctuary from which they can escape life's pressures. This approach, with its associations of sun, holiday and relaxation, creates a perfect refuge.

THEY ARE EASY TO MAINTAIN

Don't be concerned that this is a high-maintenance look, with plants that need coddling and wrapping up in the winter months; quite the opposite, in fact. This book is designed to show you how to get the look with minimum effort. It is a relaxing style of gardening

RIGHT Evergreens and climbers provide an enclosed feel to this corner, which is brightened with containers of perlargoniums and lavender

that will fit readily into busy lives. The plants need far less work and watering than those used in the traditional garden designs that many of us are accustomed to, with a square or rectangle of lawn surrounded by a border of shrubs and herbaceous perennials.

THEY ARE ENVIRONMENTALLY FRIENDLY

There are also practical implications. Global warming is an established fact and the drought resistance of this kind of garden makes for an environmentally friendly approach that will help

you to sail through periods of water shortages and hosepipe bans.

THEY PROVIDE YEAR-ROUND INTEREST

One of the joys of this style of gardening is the evergreen colour and shape and hard landscaping that provides year-round interest and structure. Within this you can add a riot of spring and summer colour – using perennials for a permanent scheme, annuals for maximum difference and flexibility, or, more commonly, a mixture of both.

CHAPTER 2

Is it difficult?

Over the years, I have come to the conclusion that there is a difference between thriving and surviving – there is little point in trying to nurture plants that are going to look as if they are just hanging on. As a quick pointer to the plants you can grow successfully in your area, you can refer to a heat-zone map that illustrates the average temperatures for different regions; you will find a version of this for the USA plus an equivalent map for Europe within this chapter. However, this book is about achieving a look and there are many ways to do this, including growing plants that look as if they belong in a hot Mediterranean climate zone, even if they don't. There are either hardy choices from Mediterranean areas – sturdy bruisers that will take care of

ABOVE **The orangery at Mapperton Gardens, Dorset, in the south-west of England, overlooks flights of stairs lined with clipped topiary**

themselves – or tough 'lookalikes' that will do the job without any cosseting. You can also extend the plants you grow by creating a microclimate in your own garden. Evergreen hedges provide sheltered enclosures, shrubs and trees can form shelter belts, sunny walls are ideal for exotic climbers, and you can exploit south and south-west facing areas of your plot.

Consequently, although establishing a Mediterranean-style garden in a temperate area sounds challenging, it doesn't have to be. You can create a striking and easy-to-care-for garden that will look good all year round and fit into the smallest site or be used in a larger garden to create an individual 'room', ideal for dining and entertaining.

IN THE UK AND NORTHERN EUROPE

Although it may seem wilful to transplant this style of gardening to these areas, it actually blends in very well. Drought-resistant plants are high-impact, architectural gems, and as a result they are highly regarded in temperate regions.

ABOVE The formal Italianate gardens in the Fountain Court at Mapperton, Dorset, south-west England, were created in the 1920s in a steep valley. They are rich with topiary in box and yew, statues dating from the nineteenth century, and this imposing pergola

THE IMPACT OF GLOBAL WARMING

Sadly, the traditional planting of temperate areas is under threat, and there will be pressure for more drought-tolerant species to be grown.

In 2002, a report commissioned by the National Trust and the Royal Horticultural Society in Great Britain pointed to a future where the beloved lawn of temperate areas becomes unsustainable during the twenty-first century. Dry summers will result in hosepipe bans and lawnless gardens unless Mediterranean species like Bermuda or Saint Augustine grasses are used.

In October 2003, an Impacts of Climate Change on Horticulture symposium was held in Providence, Rhode Island, USA, prompted by the well-recorded shift in the first-leaf and first-bloom dates of plants over the past several decades in the USA and western Europe. Experts from the USA and across the world discussed the implications for farms, orchards and gardens.

During 2004, The RHS Science Exchange, held in London, England, brought together leading horticultural scientists to discuss the future of gardening in the twenty-first century. Dr Thornton-Wood, the society's head of science, said that there was evidence to suggest there would be some frost-free winters during this century and that the landscape of much of the southern UK will be altered forever by climate change.

However, this should not be a cause for panic. Instead, gardeners should see it as an opportunity to introduce some different plants to their schemes.

TYPICAL PLANT HARDINESS ZONES FOR WESTERN EUROPE

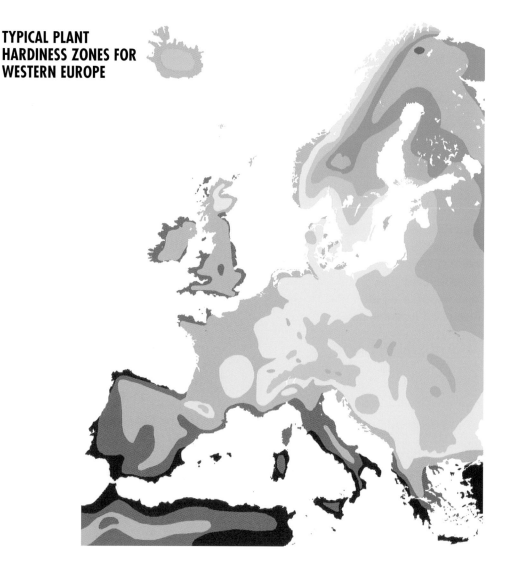

It may seem arbitrary to use plants that have originated in such different conditions but it is worth bearing in mind that you will find Mediterranean gardens ablaze with what is considered temperate 'summer bedding' – salvias, busy lizzies, petunias and zonal pelargoniums (pot geraniums) – despite the fact that watering them there is expensive and time-consuming. This means that when establishing a Mediterranean garden, it is still possible to have a blaze of summer annuals which, thankfully, needs far less attention in temperate areas than in the south of France, Spain and Italy.

IN THE USA

In North America there are more extreme variations of temperature than there are in the United Kingdom and Northern Europe. Growing Mediterranean-climate plants successfully means that you need to take into account a number of factors, including how many hours of cold weather there are in winter, how hot the summers are and whether the climate is damp or dry.

Many areas in the USA have a so-called continental climate, where the large land mass and the great distance of some places from the sea mean that there are temperature extremes as

TYPICAL PLANT HARDINESS ZONES FOR NORTH AMERICA

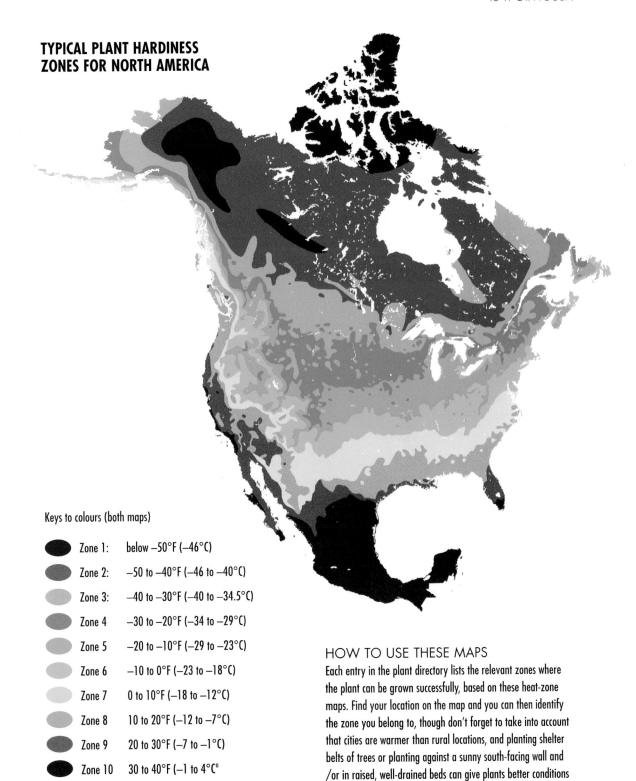

Keys to colours (both maps)

- Zone 1: below −50°F (−46°C)
- Zone 2: −50 to −40°F (−46 to −40°C)
- Zone 3: −40 to −30°F (−40 to −34.5°C)
- Zone 4: −30 to −20°F (−34 to −29°C)
- Zone 5: −20 to −10°F (−29 to −23°C)
- Zone 6: −10 to 0°F (−23 to −18°C)
- Zone 7: 0 to 10°F (−18 to −12°C)
- Zone 8: 10 to 20°F (−12 to −7°C)
- Zone 9: 20 to 30°F (−7 to −1°C)
- Zone 10: 30 to 40°F (−1 to 4°C°)
- Zone 11: above 40°F (above 4°C)

HOW TO USE THESE MAPS

Each entry in the plant directory lists the relevant zones where the plant can be grown successfully, based on these heat-zone maps. Find your location on the map and you can then identify the zone you belong to, though don't forget to take into account that cities are warmer than rural locations, and planting shelter belts of trees or planting against a sunny south-facing wall and /or in raised, well-drained beds can give plants better conditions in which to thrive.

the land mass warms up and cools down dramatically, and the climate is relatively dry. These areas of the USA have hot summers and cold winters.

As a result, many parts of the US are mild or warm and often dry, but they can be extremely cold in the winter. However, in dry areas many Mediterranean-climate plants will survive short periods of very low temperatures if the average winter temperature is not too bad. Hot summer weather also gives high sugar content to the sap, which elevates the freezing point and gives protection from winter cold.

These conditions can be more favourable than those in milder, but rainier, areas, such as the damp 'maritime climate' of seaboard regions where the body of water prevents the land from cooling down or warming beyond certain limits. It is often wet rather than cold that damages or destroys plants, as in habitat the plants can be cold but dry, so in this case planting in an

elevated position, with sharp drainage and perhaps some overhead protection will all help you to keep your garden looking good.

There are constraints even in California, where you have the same climate as the Mediterranean basin in Europe, and where all the plants from that climate zone will flourish. Because summers are so hot and dry, many plants rest in the summer. This means that without an abundant water supply the Mediterranean garden can be summer-deciduous and therefore at its worst in what is the best growing period in a temperate area.

Plants are pretty adaptable but they dislike sudden surprises! So, actually, cool weather in the autumn (fall) and in the spring will suit them better, as they will gradually enter dormancy and then begin to grow again in spring. In the UK, for example, gardeners often mourn their lost spring blossom when a sudden frost checks initial growth. Equally, in the south-east of the US

ABOVE **This USA garden with its cacti and succulents is a prototype for drought-resistant gardens in the Mediterranean basin**

the spring heats up fast, but there are no mountains to protect the Gulf of Mexico from a sudden inrush of damagingly cold arctic air.

Furthermore, the heat zones relate only to the minimum temperatures but not to how long-lasting these cold spells are, so if you have a climate zone with prolonged cold during the day or night you are much more restricted, although in really cold areas you can use techniques to protect the plants.

ACHIEVING THE LOOK

Hard landscaping can look severe in temperate regions. To avoid a sombre appearance there are ideas for planting to soften edges – species like erigeron in the risers of stone steps, ivy on pillars and balustrades, and lots of climbers.

The basic approach is to create a simple garden using low-maintenance plants, but if you are interested in extending your planting, you can, of course, introduce plants that need greater care and are more challenging, though you do not have to do this to get the look.

Instead, you can choose an easy life. For example, many tender perennials can be introduced year on year, either bought in as plants or grown from seed. Also, if you have a frost-free porch, conservatory or a sunny room in your house, you can have interesting pot plants in the winter months which will benefit from a spell outside in the summer, as this will toughen them and can free them from pests. The joy of this approach is that many of these plants will not need watering while they are outside, which immediately frees you up to loll around in the garden instead of toil in it!

USEFUL POINTERS

In general, avoid low-lying or exposed areas. Take advantage of the microclimates in your garden by planting in the shelter of a south or south-west wall, which blocks the wind and acts like a storage heater by holding the sun's heat and 'borrowing' escaped heat from the house.

ABOVE **David Wynne's statue of *Gaia* nestles among exotic vegetation in the Abbey Garden, Tresco, Isles of Scilly, south-west England**

For specific areas:

1. Northern Europe, the central and east coast of the USA, which have prolonged low minimum temperatures

Don't prune in autumn (fall) as any new growth will be vulnerable. Use a fertilizer with a high potassium content, as this toughens the foliage, while a nitrogen-based one will encourage soft new growth. Use a mulch with a depth of 3–6in (8–15cm) around the plants; you can also consider leaving the foliage on plants like dahlias, cannas, bananas and ornamental grasses to act as a protective coat as it dies down.

If you are really concerned, consider using horticultural fleece or bubble wrap, paper or cloth as a temporary blanket to cover vulnerable

ABOVE Palms, cacti, succulents and other exotic plants thrive in the mild maritime climate of Tresco's Abbey Garden in the Isles of Scilly

ABOVE The exciting desert-wash garden at East Ruston Old Vicarage, Norfolk, in the east of England, supports agaves, aloes, palms and cacti

plants during cold spells. Make sure, though, that you remove any impermeable material like polythene or bubble wrap every morning, as it will create condensation underneath as the plant warms up.

You can construct a mini glasshouse or cold frame from clear plastic or glass sheets. With the advice of a qualified electrician you can consider running heating wires through the beds. Plants can also be wrapped up or moved into a conservatory or greenhouse.

2. Low minimum temperatures for short periods, also high autumn (fall) temperatures, and high spring temperatures with spring frosts, like the southern USA

For cold protection, use a potassium fertilizer as in example 1, along with mulches and temporary blankets. Try adding sand to the soil, as it will warm up much faster after a cold spell than a heavier soil (this does not work in areas with prolonged cold). Because there is a prolonged dormant stage in the spring, delay pruning and do not fertilize until the danger of frost has passed.

3. Low autumn (fall) temperatures and/or short, low summer heat, like north-west USA and Canada and Northern Europe

Plants grow slowly so they are not large enough to overwinter; in this case give them plenty of feed in the growing season, both a slow-release fertilizer and liquid feed, and remove old leaves in spring.

4. Wet winters like the USA Pacific north-west and Northern Europe

Consider creating a waterproof canopy in the winter or planting under a covered pergola; use raised, sloping sharply drained beds. Protect the 'collar' of the plant, where the stem and root system meet, by keeping it clear of the soil and pouring a good layer of fine gravel around it so that it drains quickly.

BUT WHAT ABOUT THE WILDLIFE?

But is this a wildlife-friendly style of planting? We are all increasingly aware of the problems faced by wildlife, and in the past there has been a lot of pressure on us to use native species wherever possible. However, English Nature, the body that advises the British Government on conservation issues, is urging us to make sure that we include plants in our gardens that can survive hot spells and dry periods to make sure that there is a constant source of food for native insects, birds and butterflies. A Mediterranean area in your garden is ideal for this. (*The Times*, 21 May 2004, quoting Dr Chris Gibson, the senior policy officer of English Nature in Essex England.)

ABOVE **A bee explores the brilliant flowers of** *Opuntia compressa*, **a hardy cactus which flowers profusely every summer**

SECTION 2

LEFT Renishaw Hall,
Sheffield, north England

29

CHAPTER 3

Formal gardens

The Mediterranean garden has had a long history of reflecting the style of the formal Renaissance gardens that developed from the fourteenth century to the eighteenth century and influenced garden design for centuries after that. Originally, they themselves were believed to echo the designs that the Romans had first developed in the second century BC. These gardens spread from Italy into France and the rest of Europe; in Britain the artificial natural landscape of the renowned landscape gardener Capability Brown and his contemporaries swept this formality away, but the style held sway for much longer in the rest of Europe and still influences garden design there today.

In the south of Spain, where Moorish invasion introduced ideas from the eastern Mediterranean from the eighth century AD to the fall of Seville and Cordova in the thirteenth century, there was also the influence of Islamic gardens incorporating the concept of the *chahar bagh*, which means 'fourfold garden', the Islamic courtyard with a fountain or pool in the centre. This division has a spiritual dimension, springing from the ancient Persians' belief that the universe was divided into four quarters by a cross, with a spring of life at its centre. The four parts of the gardens represented the sacred elements of fire, air, earth and water.

There were also practical considerations, with the need for shade from relentless sunshine, so you see pergolas, arches and shady arbours that give protection from intense light and heat, and offer privacy.

GARDEN DESIGNS
TYPICAL BACKYARD

This is a particularly useful look for small front gardens, back gardens in late nineteenth- and early twentieth-century terraces, and for the small plots in modern housing developments where the enclosure provides much-welcomed privacy. It also works as a subdivision in a larger garden or backyard: perhaps a dining/barbecue/play area near the house or as an attractive solution to fill in those awkward spaces in the right-angles of buildings.

There are two approaches to designing a garden in a small plot like this. Either, as illustrated, you can use the space as a paved outside 'room', with an area for seating and for children to play in, a space for storing gardening equipment, and with planting confined to narrow borders, climbers on walls or fences and containers of flowering plants.

Alternatively, you can use the narrow arm of the 'L' as an entrance (or as a pergola for climbers if the area is sunny). Then choose one of the other plans, shown on pages 32, 37, or 70, for the remaining square.

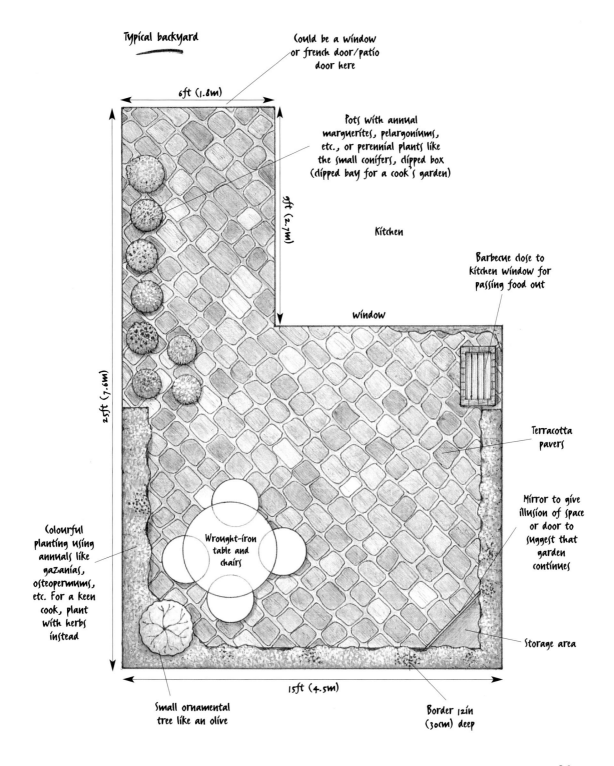

Typical backyard

Could be a window or french door/patio door here

6ft (1.8m)

9ft (2.7m)

Pots with annual marguerites, pelargoniums, etc., or perennial plants like the small conifers, clipped box (clipped bay for a cook's garden)

Kitchen

Barbecue close to kitchen window for passing food out

window

25ft (7.6m)

Terracotta pavers

Colourful planting using annuals like gazanias, osteopermums, etc. For a keen cook, plant with herbs instead

Wrought-iron table and chairs

Mirror to give illusion of space or door to suggest that garden continues

Storage area

15ft (4.5m)

Small ornamental tree like an olive

Border 12in (30cm) deep

AXIAL COURTYARD
WITH HARD LANDSCAPING

This plan illustrates the basic structure for an elaborately constructed paved area with four beds, and it gives you an infinitely expandable formal and geometrical structure. The scale is based on 18in (46cm) square paving slabs but can be adapted to other-sized areas by adding or removing slabs or changing the size of the paving slabs used.

It is based on an axial plan with lots of right angles. Straight paths end in focal points. If you have a big garden you might have a viewpoint out over the surrounding countryside; otherwise this garden is inward-looking. Statues, water features, armillary spheres, or perhaps a modern piece you have chosen, made or discovered, will all help to give the right impression. The other essential element is that of containment; these gardens have an enclosed feel. This can be achieved in a number of ways, including the use of clipped hedges, walls, and trellis over fences. In larger spaces you are looking for subdivisions, and in any size of space, pergolas and arbours will give you shade and privacy.

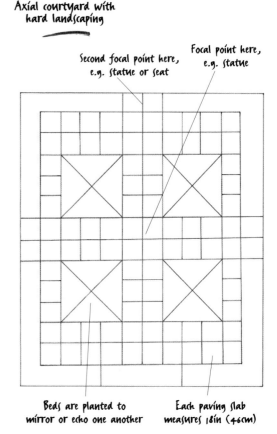

Axial courtyard with hard landscaping

Second focal point here, e.g. statue or seat

Focal point here, e.g. statue

Beds are planted to mirror or echo one another

Each paving slab measures 18in (46cm)

ABOVE This fourfold, geometrical courtyard has a chubby, clipped box ball in each quarter. This design would look good as the centrepiece of a small backyard with seating off to one side, or as a scheme for a small front garden

A. Sensory garden with a formal structure

This design was created as a memorial garden to Mrs Jean Smith, a school governor and county councillor who worked hard for our local primary school.

It is intended as a sensory garden, where children can escape alone or in pairs for some peace and solitude, and to enjoy the sounds, scent, look, feel and even taste of the garden (as it uses culinary herbs for some of the planting).

Sensory garden

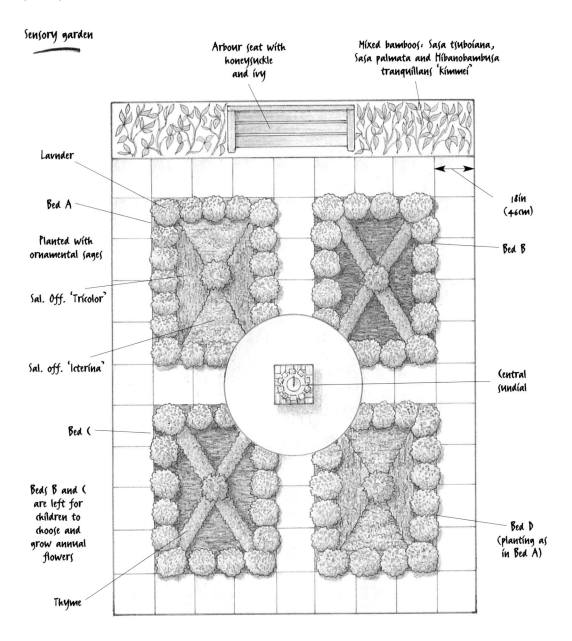

Arbour seat with honeysuckle and ivy

Mixed bamboos: Sasa tsuboiana, Sasa palmata and Hibanobambusa tranquillans 'kimmei'

Lavnder

Bed A

Planted with ornamental sages

Sal. Off. 'Tricolor'

Sal. off. 'Icterina'

18in (46cm)

Bed B

Central sundial

Bed C

Beds B and C are left for children to choose and grow annual flowers

Bed D (planting as in Bed A)

Thyme

ABOVE In practice, the garden evolved from this original design. As the paths were made wider for wheelchair access, it was felt there was insufficient space for a sundial, and obelisks were placed in the centre of each bed. The final garden design can be seen overleaf

ABOVE **The paving in the finished memorial garden was modified for easy wheelchair access so that all the children can enjoy it**

The garden has a formal structure, using hard landscaping to produce geometrical beds that are planted with colourful scented herbs like lavender and variegated sage around tall central obelisks, which are used to support a mix of flowering climbers. The herb beds have been block-planted for evergreen colour and the minimum of care.

It has an arbour seat, made from recycled materials, which will also be draped in climbers, and a hedge that will grow to surround and enclose the hard landscaping so that the garden will be a private refuge.

All the planting is designed to be at its best in the spring and early summer while the children are at school.

In addition, the paths have been altered from the original design and made particularly wide, as wheelchair access is mandatory for a public garden like this.

Bamboos are used as a boundary between the garden and the road outside. This gives privacy and also an evergreen backdrop, with the constantly murmuring and rustling sound of leaves for relaxation. The species used are *Sasa tsuboiana*, which reaches 5–6½ft (1.5–2m) in

their own plants from seed, using quick colourful annuals like marigolds, candytuft and petunias for flowers. In the final garden, obelisks were used and climbers like sweet peas and morning glories could be grown. Or, to emphasise the sensory aspect with 'taste', they could grow runner beans on the obelisks and quick-and-easy vegetables like radishes and lettuces in the beds.

LEFT Each of the school children decorated a tile, which was then fired. In the original plan, one of my ideas was for the tiles to be used together to form a panel at the back of the arbour seat

RIGHT Sturdy metal obelisks with attractive tops or finials are decorative in their own right and act as a support to climbing plants. They also make a good central focal point for each of the little beds

height and has large, dark-green leaves that grow to 10in (25cm) long, combined with fast-growing *Sasa palmata*, which reaches the same height and has wide green leaves on arching stems and a curving habit with layers of leaves. For a flickering effect, these were used in conjunction with the smaller, variegated *Hibanobambusa tranquillans* 'kimmei'. This has dark-green leaves with yellow stripes on short slender stems, and reaches a height of 3–6½ft (91cm–2m).

Because this is a children's garden, two of the little beds, B and C on the plan on page 33, could be given to the children for them to grow

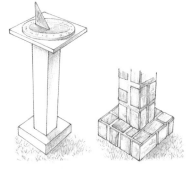

LEFT Another idea to involve the children in the garden project was to use their tiles to cover the base of a sundial to create a colourful centrepiece

ABOVE **This is a useful culinary formal garden with beds filled with herbs and walled with espalier pear trees**

B. An 'edible' formal garden with hard landscaping, box hedging, and espalier pears
This garden uses box to enclose a riotous planting of herbs, surrounded by espalier pear trees. In a small garden, herbs are one of the most useful choices for the cook, as you have the advantage of freshness and constancy of supply along with the opportunity to select unusual and exciting species to grow, which may otherwise be difficult to source. You can also try Mediterranean vegetables like peppers and courgettes, with outside tomatoes and perhaps runner beans grown as ornamental centrepieces on obelisks.

C. A simple courtyard
Many houses have a dead space in the right angle of walls alongside extensions, garages and outbuildings. These areas can work for you. In this case the walls create a sheltered suntrap for an outside dining space that is close to the kitchen, so the cook doesn't have too much running around to do. Containers of summer bedding plants are added to cordylines in containers, and the walls will eventually have an overcoat of climbing plants.

ABOVE **This sheltered courtyard is ideal for summer bedding and container displays of palms, citrus and other exotics**

FOURFOLD GEOMETRICAL BEDS WITH AXIAL PATHS

In this design, each slab represents the standard 18in (46cm) square paving slab; the overall plot is 10ft (3m) across by 12ft (3.6m) deep, but it can easily be altered by adding or subtracting slabs or using larger or smaller slabs.

One of the most ubiquitous Mediterranean looks is the formal and geometrical garden, with lots of hard landscaping and repetition of features such as clipped evergreen hedges and topiary, for example, or matched containers with mirror planting. There is always a strong focal point, like a statue, dovecote, armillary sphere, interesting tiling, a water feature, or topiary.

Although this is an apparently rigid and constrictive form of gardening, it has the benefit of being one of the easiest schemes to lay out, and it will accommodate anything from the most minimal planting to contrastingly lavish and blowsy planting that serve to soften the rigid axial plan. This means that it can change radically from season to season and from year to year, so you will never tire of it.

We all have to stretch our finances to accommodate the things we need, let alone the things we want. If you haven't got a huge budget, then this little garden is designed to be built for the least cost possible, using cast slabs and gravel for the hard landscaping.

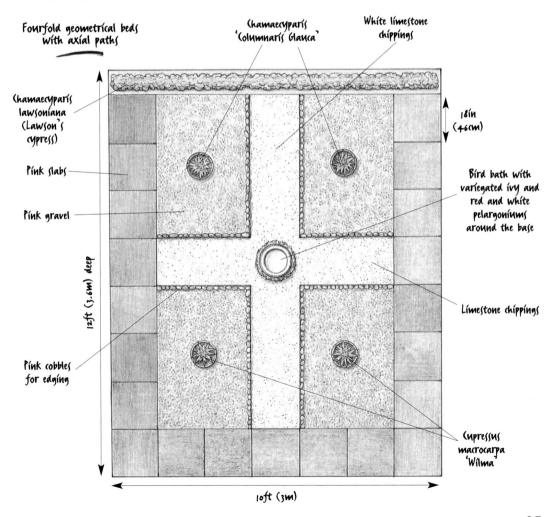

Fourfold geometrical beds with axial paths

Chamaecyparis 'Columnaris Glauca'

White limestone chippings

Chamaecyparis lawsoniana (Lawson's cypress)

Pink slabs

Pink gravel

Bird bath with variegated ivy and red and white pelargoniums around the base

12ft (3.6m) deep

Limestone chippings

Pink cobbles for edging

Cupressus macrocarpa 'Wilma'

18in (46cm)

10ft (3m)

ABOVE *Agave americana* 'Variegata', back, and *Agave americana* 'Mediopicta Alba', front, against a Lawson cypress hedge

ABOVE Containers of marguerites, *Leucanthemum vulgare*, surround a bird bath underplanted with pelargoniums and ivy

This design recreates the geometrical formality of a Mediterranean garden surrounded by walling or hedging, plus hard landscaping, and it can be adapted to any square or rectangular geometrical space.

In two versions of the scheme, the focal point is a bird bath, which cost less than a takeaway Indian meal for two. Judicious use of the yoghurt mixture for instant ageing (see Section 3, 'Style on a budget', page 107, for instruction on the technique) will give the piece a romantic, ruinous look like the real thing, if preferred.

Of course, you may well have a larger budget, in which case the sky is the limit, both for your choice of hard landscaping or for an architectural centrepiece, which might be a high-quality reproduction, a genuine older piece, or a special piece of sculpture. Driftwood, found on a local beach or by a river, can make interesting features or, more formally, you can buy Natural Driftwood Sculptures, which are Canadian western-red-cedar pieces, remnants of the lumber industry that have been immersed and naturally river-moulded for over 70 years. Pieces of weathered stone are sculptures in their own right, or they could be drilled to make an exciting and unusual water feature. Quarries or reclamation yards can also be very rewarding sources of interesting objects. In every case, in a front garden it is advisable to cement the structure into place if you are likely to be plagued by light-fingered passers-by.

The garden is bounded by a hedge of the ubiquitous Lawson cypress *Chamaecyparis lawsoniana* (syn. *Cupressus lawsoniana*). This makes a virtue of necessity, in that this is often the hedging of choice in terms of speed of growth and privacy, though it goes without saying after the equal ubiquity of neighbourly, or rather unneighbourly, lawsuits that it needs to be kept under control. However, it makes a wonderful

formal backdrop and is reminiscent of the less hardy Mediterranean cypress (Italian cyprus or *Cupressus sempervirens*, or Californian or Monterey cyprus *C. macrocarpa*). Any evergreen hedging or walling would be an equally appropriate backdrop.

The whole garden is constructed over a layer of permeable membrane, laid on a well-levelled and compacted base. The membrane will prevent any weeds from appearing from the underlying soil while allowing free drainage. Any weed growth you encounter will be lightly rooted into the surface material and can therefore be readily removed; in dry spells you will find there is no weeding required at all.

The axial path is constructed of white limestone chippings, edged with pink cobbles. The tiny beds are dressed with pink gravel and surrounded with raspberry-pink paving stones, though the scheme could use a variety of hard-landscaping materials that would give a totally different look, such as terracotta paving and terracotta roped edging with a mixed gravel in tones of sand, gold and terracotta. Dark slabs and edging with plum or blue slate chippings would also look austere and effective.

The planting can follow a number of approaches, such as using terracotta pots of contrasting pairs of conifers. *Chamaecyparis*

RIGHT *Chamaecyparis* 'Columnaris Glauca' and a golden *Cupressus macrocarpa* 'Wilma' with an 'instant topiary' pillar

'Columnaris Glauca' makes a compact blue-grey pyramid, and the aromatic golden *Cupressus macrocarpa* 'Wilma' is a faster-growing golden-yellow conifer, but again it can be kept trimmed to shape. In the summer, you could have a complete change by planting around the conifers with colourful flowering annuals, such as a tumbling mass of trailing zonal pelargoniums, for example, or easy-care impatiens. Compact hardy palms in Versailles tubs, like *Chamaerops*

LEFT This attractive herb garden at Ayscoughfee Hall and Gardens in Spalding, Lincolnshire, east England, has a mature central bay tree (*Laurus nobilis*) surrounded by beds spilling lavender, thymes, sage and other aromatics over warm-coloured brick paths

the fabulous blue palm, *Brahea armata*; in winter they could move into a porch, conservatory or even the garage if kept dry. Large half-hardy variegated *Agave americana* 'Variegata' or *Agave americana* 'Mediopicta Alba' would also make a showy display if you have winter quarters for them.

In one version of this garden, the plinth of the bird bath has ivy garlands added which will enhance it as the plant grows; in the summer you can add pot geraniums (pelargoniums) to add softness and colour to the scheme. For a change, fill the pots with more pelargoniums or with marguerites, *Leucanthemum vulgare*, which will flower all summer.

Topiary is another option. Balls, cones, spires and pyramids of *Buxus sempervirens*, or common box, look stylish and only need trimming once or twice a year to keep them in shape. Topiary can also be an alternative centrepiece. However, even a metre or so trimmed shape will cost you the equivalent of a good meal for two, so you may want to think about a pillar or post covered with a tousle of variegated ivy like the 'instant' ivy topiary cheats seen in Section 3 instead (see page 104).

ALTERNATIVE FOURFOLD PLANTING

Because the previous design is a garden based on four quarters, each mirroring the others, it is an easy scheme to customize to your own tastes, as can be seen in the following two designs.

A. Herb bed

The design shown on page 42 is based on one quarter of a fourfold herb bed. Width 46in (117cm); depth 55in (140cm).

One of the most evocative of the senses is the sense of smell: a whole world of experience can

humilis or the dwarf windmill palm, *Trachycarpus wagnerianus*, would also be very effective. In a larger space, *T. fortunei* would make an impressive show in big containers. In the summer, you could try less-hardy *Phoenix canariensis* or

41

Fourfold herb bed

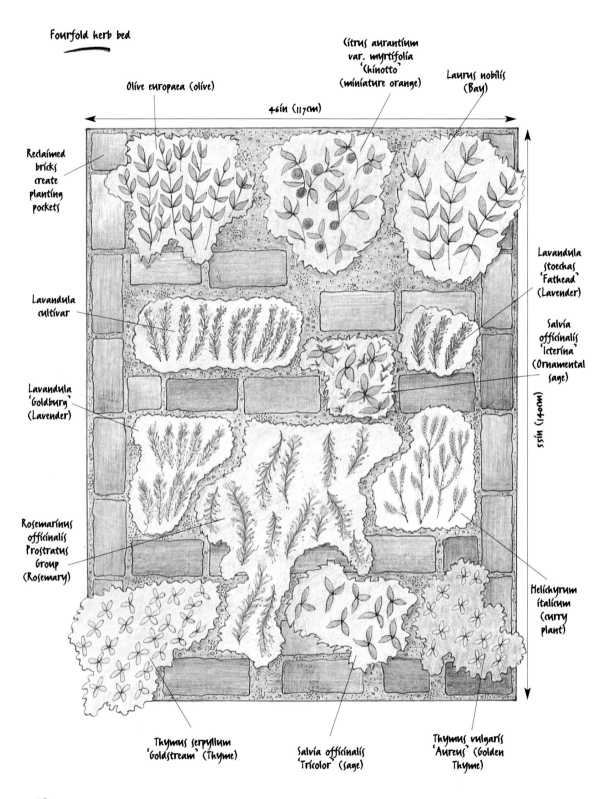

Olíve europaea (olive)

Citrus aurantium
var. myrtifolia
'Chinotto'
(miniature orange)

Laurus nobilis
(Bay)

46in (117cm)

Reclaimed
bricks
create
planting
pockets

Lavandula
stoechas
'Fathead'
(Lavender)

Lavandula
cultivar

Salvia
officinalis
'Icterina'
(Ornamental
sage)

Lavandula
'Goldburg'
(Lavender)

55in (140cm)

Rosemarinus
officinalis
Prostratus
Group
(Rosemary)

Helichyrum
italicum
(curry
plant)

Thymus serpyllum
'Goldstream' (Thyme)

Salvia officinalis
'Tricolor' (Sage)

Thymus vulgaris
'Aureus' (Golden
Thyme)

ABOVE The exotics in the back row (see plan on page 42) will remain compact in containers (and can be overwintered under glass if necessary) but if given a free root run they will need more space. The other herbs can be kept in check by regular clipping

be conjured up by a whiff of your mother's favourite perfume, baby talcum powder, freshly brewed coffee and, of course, the aromatic herbs of the Mediterranean. It is a fragrance redolent of sunshine, blue skies, warm sea and leisure. What could be nicer than to walk up your path and into your house surrounded by such suggestive scents! A lavender-edged pathway to a front door, for instance, is a wonderful welcome, both to the weary home-comer and to the visitor, and it makes for a colourful and long-lasting summer display.

Just like ornamental grasses, the creeping herbs are an excellent choice when you want something to soften the severity of an otherwise rigid garden. They make an invaluable addition to a front garden that is mainly made up of hard landscaping. Taller varieties can sprawl over the wall, while the smaller thymes can scramble among the paving. They also work very well in formal containers and make a winning combination with clipped box hedges, where again they serve to soften the austere angularity.

43

ABOVE **Native Mediterranean flora tends to show its evolutionary drought resistance by outward signals, such as its possession of grey foliage, like the pungent-leaved *Helichrysum italicum*, the so-called curry plant, or by its shiny evergreen leaves, like those of the sweet bay, *Laurus nobilis***

Although the fourfold garden plan on page 42 illustrates a really tiny plot, it is the kind of bed that could be doubled in size, then doubled or quadrupled, to give two or four beds with little brick-lined paths running between them for access. This would provide a successful symmetrical scheme, with each bed either echoing or ringing the changes slightly on the other or others.

This is an aromatic planting, using a mixture of variegated herbs for maximum colour and texture, and one that makes a virtue out of a problem, too. The plan was designed to colonize old foundations at the foot of a barn wall. As a result, the impoverished soil in this forcibly raised bed and its position against a heat-storing south-facing wall is ideal.

In milder areas you can also use a south-facing wall to provide shelter to the more borderline planting. *Olea europaea*, the European olive, with its silver foliage and tiny white spring flowers, is much hardier than is often believed, although it won't usually ripen fruit in temperate zones. *Citrus aurantium* var. *myrtifolia* 'Chinotto', the miniature orange, is also perfectly happy in a sheltered spot, although both the olive and citrus make unusual and pretty houseplants, especially the citrus, which magically can be in flower and fruit simultaneously – so you can always use these as summer container 'extras'.

The herbs in this tiny garden have a dual purpose in that they are suitable for culinary use, though the more ornamental cultivars with variegated leaves have been chosen for maximum impact, such as the gold and green *Salvia officinalis* 'Icterina', the purple, white and green sage *Salvia officinalis* 'Tricolor' and the colourful thymes like the golden thyme and *Thymus serpyllum* 'Goldstream'. They will automatically be kept in check if used for cooking, otherwise give each plant a firm cutting back after flowering so that the design doesn't get out of hand.

For flowers, there are numerous pretty lavender cultivars, with flowers in shades of white, pink and mauve, and large-flowered cultivars such as *Lavandula stoechas* 'Fathead'. There are also cultivars with pretty leaves, such as the showy gold and green variegated leaves of *Lavandula* 'Burgoldeen' syn. *Lavandula* 'Goldburg'.

Rosemary is also good for flower, both in the normal blue-flowered true species and in its white- and pink-flowered cultivars. In addition, there is a very attractive scrambling form, named *Rosmarinus officinalis* Prostratus Group, which will hang beautifully over walls and down steps.

ABOVE Ornamental grasses are effective in borders and containers, either alone or used as a contrast to other plants. They are particularly valuable for their range of foliage colour and for their arching and sometimes billowing forms, so a mixture of these plants can be used to make striking grass gardens, which look especially good when contrasted with severe formal landscaping, as shown

B. Ornamental grasses with formal paving

Scale: 6ft (1.8m) across and 7ft (2.1m) deep; each small paving slab measures 8 x 4in (20 x 10cm).

Ornamental grasses, so redolent of the hot and dry areas of the world, play an important role with their strong forms and shapes, though the lax and sprawling appearance of some

grasses, and the spreading habit of a number of more invasive species, can deter people from using these architectural gems. However, they do lend themselves well to the creation of striking and easy-to-care-for garden or patio areas, with year-round interest and the minimum of maintenance and watering required. Some grasses can be invasive, or

45

ABOVE **These small 8 x 4in (20 x 10cm) pavers can be laid out with ready-made planting pockets for your choice of grasses**

they self-seed readily, so if they are confined by hard landscaping they cannot run wild, and the contrast of hard materials with the softer and often weeping forms of the grasses is very effective.

At its simplest, planting into gravel gives a low-cost but striking arrangement, and chunks of blue slate, rounded cobbles and other natural structures can complement both the gravel and the grasses. They can also soften what could otherwise be sparse expanses of wooden decking and set off other planting. They are especially good for displaying statuary.

This little garden gives you the best of both worlds. The grasses are forcibly contained within rectangular, square and L-shaped planting pockets in paved hard landscaping in warm terracotta. Meanwhile, the contrasting soft weeping foliage, the architectural forms and exciting colours are set off in all their glory. The planting uses a backdrop of taller

miscanthus, including, left to right on page 45, slender-leaved *Miscanthus sinensis* 'Morning Light', also known as Chinese silver grass, which forms upright clumps of white-edged, bright-green foliage and *Miscanthus sinensis* 'Zebrinus', the distinctive hardy zebra grass, which has slender mid-green leaves with unusual and very attractive horizontal banding and sprays of pretty pinkish-brown flowers in the autumn (fall). *Stipa arundinacea*, with its loosely tufted dark-green leaves, streaked orange-brown in summer and turning orange-brown all winter, is planted behind the silvery-green arching leaves of *Carex comans* 'Frosted Curls'. In the middle is *Carex phyllocephala* 'Sparkler', which is very brightly variegated with strong white margins and produces spiralling whorls of pointed leaves on erect stems. It makes an attractive contrast to *Carex buchananii* on the right, with its bronze, arching leaves.

46

Ornamental grasses with
formal paving

*The height of the
planting decreases
from the back row
to the front

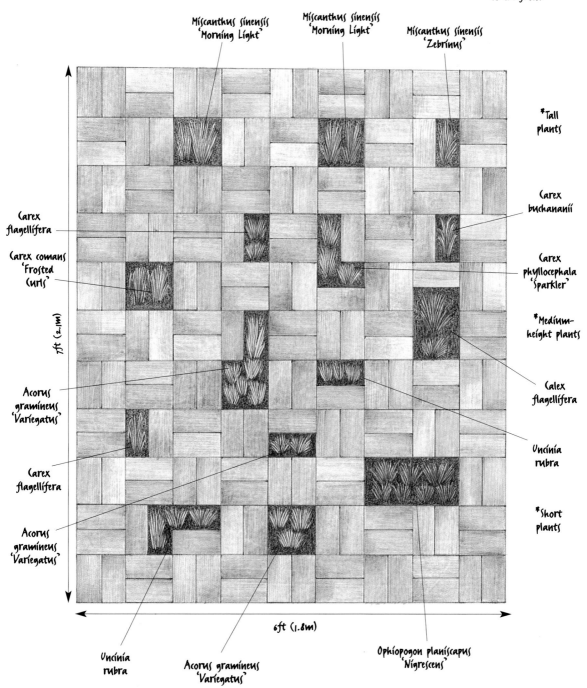

Miscanthus sinensis
'Morning Light'

Miscanthus sinensis
'Morning Light'

Miscanthus sinensis
'Zebrinus'

*Tall
plants

Carex
buchananii

Carex
flagellifera

Carex comans
'Frosted
Curls'

Carex
phyllocephala
'Sparkler'

*Medium-
height plants

Acorus
gramineus
'Variegatus'

Calex
flagellifera

7ft (2.1m)

Carex
flagellifera

Uncinia
rubra

Acorus
gramineus
'Variegatus'

*Short
plants

6ft (1.8m)

Uncinia
rubra

Acorus gramineus
'Variegatus'

Ophiopogon planiscapus
'Nigrescens'

Ideas for alternative grass gardens

ABOVE This scheme in Lincolnshire, east England, shows that in hard landscaping you can use any mixed planting, with or instead of ornamental grasses to soften and contrast with rigid geometrical lines

ABOVE The formal garden at Pine Lodge Gardens and Nursery, St Austell, Cornwall, in the south-west of England, was paved with over 8,000 granite cobbles recycled from a station platform; grasses were used as a soft, informal contrast

ABOVE In this style of gardening the hard landscaping is just as important a part of the garden as the actual planting. Here the flowing lines and the different colours and materials in the paving and the softly weeping grasses enhance each other

ABOVE *Phyllostachys nigra* and *Phyllostachys aurea*, the black and the golden bamboos, reach about 15ft (4.6m) in time, but they are clumping species so they never spread out of control. The barrels contain *Trachycarpus fortunei*, a hardy palm that is always shapely

DECKING SCHEMES

We all love the idea of a secret garden, a quiet sanctuary where we can retreat to read a book, drink a cup of coffee or just take a few minutes out to relax and unwind. A front garden can be a secluded oasis, or a patio can be tucked into the angles of a house to create a private refuge. The first prerequisite is a seat, which can vary from the functional to the bizarre.

Although decking is less popular than it was, it is quick and relatively inexpensive to install, and it does give clean modern lines which complement bamboos and grasses, and even allows for cut-out areas which function as integral water features.

A focal point gives added interest when daydreaming or sitting, though the element of choice for most of us is probably going to be moving water. There are lots of small features which are soothing to watch and listen to,

ranging from the traditional through to the more unusual. Many need only the minimum amount of water, so they are safe for homes with tiny children, for whom water can be dangerously attractive.

A. Decking patio with palms in wooden barrels and a bamboo backdrop

Each square of decking measures 20in (51cm), so the decking patio is 10ft across x 6ft deep (3 x 1.8m); the wooden bench is 4ft (1.2m) wide and the tubs each have a diameter of 2ft (61cm).

This scheme offers a private retreat with a tucked-away seat. It could stand alone or be combined with an enclosed, almost jungle-like planting of bamboos and palms or with hardy architecturals, plus a little water feature in each case as a focal point (see page 52 for an example of it combined with scheme B).

Decking patio with palms in wooden
barrels and a bamboo backdrop

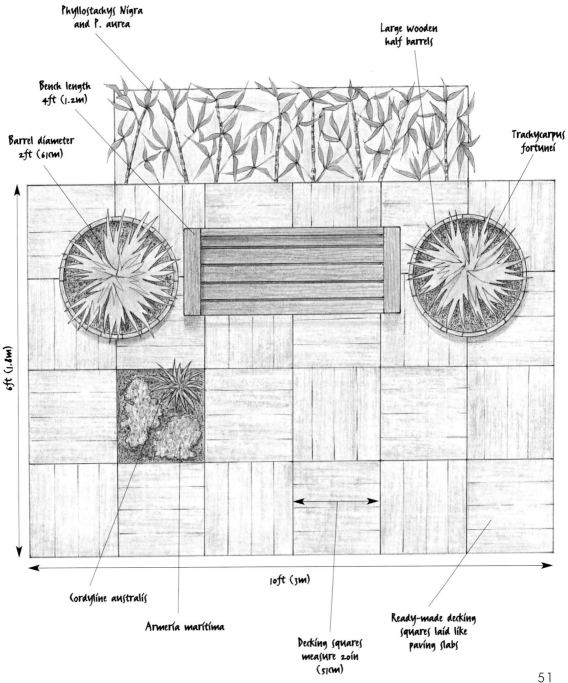

Phyllostachys Nigra
and P. aurea

Large wooden
half barrels

Bench length
4ft (1.2m)

Barrel diameter
2ft (61cm)

Trachycarpus
fortunei

6ft (1.8m)

10ft (3m)

Cordyline australis

Armeria maritima

Decking squares
measure 20in
(51cm)

Ready-made decking
squares laid like
paving slabs

51

The backdrop to the decking and the bench is a combined planting of *Phyllostachys nigra* and *Phyllostachys aurea*, the black and the golden bamboos, respectively, so there is an interesting flickering between dark and light in the stems. Elegant and shapely, these plants will grow to about 15ft (4.6m) tall, but you can trim them to a lower height if you prefer. They are probably the best bamboos you can choose for specimen planting: they are clump-forming, which means that they have a graceful, almost fountain-like arching form; they will not run riot in your garden like some species; they keep their leaves through winter (but shed leaves during the growing season as the new growth comes so, sadly,

ABOVE **Scheme A is combined with scheme B to make a pretty patio or courtyard area with secluded seating facing a small water feature against a backdrop of mixed architectural specimens**

there is leaf-fall to collect!); and they stand incredible battering from gale-force wind without ending up as bald sticks. Indeed, to the Chinese they are a symbol of endurance in that they bend but do not break, so they have a spiritual dimension too.

Other possibilities with a similar habit of growth include *Phyllostachys nigra* 'Boryana' and *Phyllostachys edulis*. All the bamboos are excellent for creating what you could call a dappled privacy, so that you have shade and protection from prying eyes without feeling that you are hemmed in by something looming and dark (like Lawson cypress!).

Clumping bamboos spread out from where you plant them, but others are much sneakier and more invasive, and will appear all over the place. Plant the non-clumping species in large containers, sunk in the ground, to confine them.

I always think that bamboos are the silver birches of the shrub world, in that they are also in constant movement, with a continuous shivering and a soft whispering of leaves that is very soothing. In a small garden this gives privacy without gloom, so this proposal is ideal for a secluded spot where you may want to sit out and enjoy the rustling of the bamboo or for a small back-garden patio.

This apparently exotic scheme looks as if it comes from the south coast of France or the Spanish costas; but again this is a fully hardy planting which can be assembled and more or less left to its own devices.

The palms in the wooden half barrels are both *Trachycarpus fortunei*, which is a fully hardy palm and also has the benefit of making a shapely specimen at every stage of its life. You have the choice of keeping the lower branches for a bushy effect or of cutting back the old growth to reveal the furry trunk. In containers, the growth is slowed down substantially unless you feed it well in the growing season; but this can obviously be a benefit if you have restricted space or if you are likely to move and to want

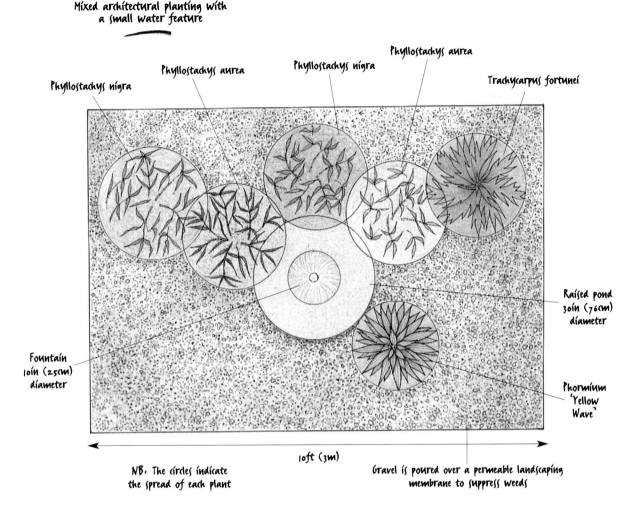

Mixed architectural planting with a small water feature

Phyllostachys nigra

Phyllostachys aurea

Phyllostachys nigra

Phyllostachys aurea

Trachycarpus fortunei

Raised pond
30in (76cm)
diameter

Fountain
10in (25cm)
diameter

Phormium
'Yellow
Wave'

10ft (3m)

NB: The circles indicate
the spread of each plant

Gravel is poured over a permeable landscaping
membrane to suppress weeds

to take what is, in all honesty, an expensive plant with you. They are very drought-tolerant, which is another advantage for a container plant, so will need relatively little care; just water them in the hottest, driest periods and add a handful of slow-release granular fertilizer each spring. For a softer look, surround the base of the trunk with a riot of summer annuals or thread a flowering climber through its branches.

B. Mixed architectural planting with a small water feature

This scheme measures 10ft (3m) across; the raised pond has a 30in (76cm) diameter and is 21in (53cm) high; the globe water feature has a 10in (25cm) diameter.

All this pro-phyllostachys publicity makes this an obvious design to combine with another scheme that has a bamboo backdrop. It has an additional planting of *Cortaderia selloana* (pampas grass) for extra height, and contrasting flamboyant ostrich-feather plumes of flower. The curving sprays of *Phormium* 'Yellow Wave' bring up a foreground of lower container planting which echoes the arching shapes of the cortaderia and phyllostachys. It also has a delightful 'secret garden' feel, with a half-hidden water feature that has water gushing over the

ABOVE **Scheme B has a child-friendly water feature, so that you can still have the sight and sound of running water in the garden**

smooth sphere in the raised pool. This means it is a safe garden for children, too, but one which retains the sound and appearance of moving water. On its own, rather than combined with the decking feature, this scheme is perfect for a front garden that runs alongside a garage and drive where another car has to be parked in front of the house, as the planting is tall enough to have impact even when all the cars are parked. Alternatively, this could be the surroundings of a back-garden patio for private dining and relaxing, or it could act as a backdrop for a foreground area with lower planting in gravel or paving.

C. Hardy alternatives or a scheme using hardy lookalikes

This scheme measures 10ft (3m) across. The black water feature has a 15in (38cm) diameter.

You may like the idea and feel of a Mediterranean-style garden, but the idea of coping with dubiously hardy plants is deterring you. Perhaps you want to plant it up and forget it, or perhaps you simply do not have anywhere

to keep plants apart from outside, where they will have to take their chances with the elements. You may live in a location which is particularly frost-prone and unfavourable to many species.

If so, the solution is to go for plants which appear more exotic than they are, creating that foreign look and feel with plants that are actually real bruisers and will accept anything our climate throws at them. Again, this scheme combines well with the decking and with hardy palms, giving an exotic impression while in reality being very tough and resilient.

Some of the large and glossy-leaved evergreens give the impression of an exotic location while tolerating anything. *Fatsia japonica* and *Fatsia japonica* 'Variegata' have large, deeply divided leaves, like expressive hands, which make a really effective backdrop. They grow to anything between 5 to 12ft (1.5 to 3.6m) height and spread, and can be pruned selectively to keep an attractive shape. In this scheme, fatsia has been used along with *Aucuba japonica*, the spotted laurel, which is reminiscent of a house plant, the much more

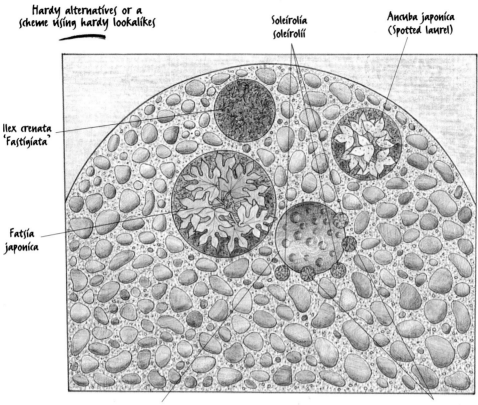

Hardy alternatives or a
scheme using hardy lookalikes

Soleirolia
soleirolii

Aucuba japonica
(Spotted laurel)

NB. The circles
indicate the
spread of each
plant

Ilex crenata
'Fastigiata'

Fatsia
japonica

Water feature – 15in (38cm) diameter. It is frost-proof pottery
stained with cobalt oxide and contains a small pump. Wiring is
under the gravel. Use a qualified electrician to install it

Ajuga reptans
'Braunherz'

exotic *Schefflera actinophylla* or umbrella tree. However, unlike schefflera, aucuba is almost ludicrously tolerant: it grows in virtually any position, including dark corners, and it is also happy in containers. There are other cultivars that are more dramatically splashed with colour, including *Aucuba japonica* 'Crotonifolia' and *Aucuba japonica* 'Golden King'. They can reach 9 x 9ft (2.7 x 2.7m) eventually but in spring can be pruned hard to size in smaller spaces. Here they have been combined with *Ilex crenata* 'Fastigiata', the box-leaved holly, which forms a dark, slender column with tiny leaves. It is slow-growing, though it can reach12–18ft (3.6–5.5m) eventually, but again the ilex can be clipped to shape if you want to keep a compact group.

ABOVE **Another child-friendly water feature, softened with *Soleirolia soleirolii* and purple-leaved *Ajuga reptans* 'Braunherz'**

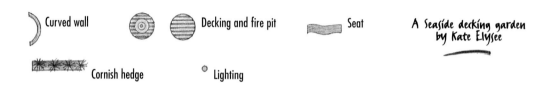

Curved wall

Decking and fire pit

Seat

*A Seaside decking garden
by Kate Elysee*

Cornish hedge

Lighting

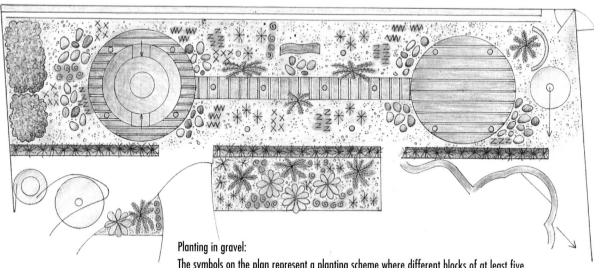

Planting in gravel:
The symbols on the plan represent a planting scheme where different blocks of at least five of each of a number of species are used, selected from Anthemis, *Armeria maritima, Crambe maritima*, erigeron, *Eryngium planum, E. varifolium, Scabious perfecta, Sedum* 'Autumn Joy', *Verbena bonariensis, Carex comans* 'Bronze', and bronze fennel, plus dotted specimen plants chosen from *Agave americana, Euphorbia mysinites, E. wulfenii* and *Yucca gloriosa* 'Variegata'

These plants all have the advantage of possessing such a distinctive shape and form that they can be used emphatically in a grouping together. Here, they are clustered around a frost-proof pottery water feature, stained almost black with cobalt oxide, which bubbles gently among a group of river-rounded cobbles. The water feature is edged with *Soleirolia soleirolii*, perhaps better known as *Helxine soleirolii* ('baby's tears' or 'mind your own business') a tiny, mat-forming creeping plant, almost indestructible, though it may lose its leaves in a cold winter. The soleirolia also comes as very pretty-coloured cultivars like *S.* 'Golden Queen' and *S.* 'Silver Queen', which could be combined in an interesting variegated edging if used alternately; however, in this case, the interplanting is with the strongly contrasting dark-bronze-leaved *Ajuga reptans* 'Braunherz', to pick up the dark leaves of the holly and the deep cobalt stain of the water feature.

Again, this small feature planting would stand alone in the tiniest patch of front garden, giving a year-round and maintenance-free solution to what could otherwise be the problem of a dead and dreary space.

D. A seaside decking garden by Kate Elysee
This interesting garden literally overlooks the beach in Poole, Dorset, south-west of England. Decking is used to provide a viewpoint area, and there is a fire pit and lots of dry planting.

The curved, painted end wall is a feature to hide an ugly gate and it has a piece of Natural Driftwood Sculpture to add a focal point which is then flanked by dramatic black aeoniums.

The planting includes:

Phoenix canariensis, Stipa arundinacea, tamarisk, *Arundo donax, Buddleja davidii* 'Black Knight', *Muehlenbeckia complexa, Agave americana,* anthemis, *Armeria maritima, Crambe maritima,* erigeron, *Eryngium planum, E. variifolium, Euphorbia myrsinites, E. characias* subsp. *wulfenii, Scabiosa caucasica* Perfecta Series, *Sedum* 'Autumn Joy', *Verbena bonariensis, Carex comans* 'Bronze', and bronze fennel.

PARTERRES

The National Trust-owned Overbecks garden, overlooking the Salcombe Estuary, Devon, in the south-west of England, was founded in 1901 by Eric Hopkins, who laid out the basic design of the garden with its small compartments and

ABOVE **Kate Elysee's garden uses a curved wall to hide an ugly gateway, which also acts as a focal point for a Natural Driftwood Sculpture, framed by black** *Aeonium arboreum* **'Zwartkop' and a date palm,** *Phoenix canariensis*

BELOW **This lovely parterre at Overbecks, Devon, in the south-west of England, has formal clipped box hedges and pots of citrus plants**

ABOVE This parterre is a wonderfully simple solution for what to do with a really small front garden, giving it structure while contrasting with a riot of colourful summer bedding

intimate garden, with lots of secret corners and surprises, like the statue garden with its riotous herbaceous borders overflowing with tender perennials which leads through pillars draped with a huge *Vitis coignetiae* to a secret garden with a massive *Phoenix canariensis*. This little compartment overlooks a parterre, which was planted in 1991. The parterre is hidden behind the working greenhouses and the gardeners' hut, with its Mediterranean-style terracotta roof tiles and blue paint, and is designed to be seen only from above. The small clipped box hedges, using *Buxus sempervirens* 'Suffruticosa', a compact dwarf form, outline a gravelled courtyard decorated with large glazed pots of orange and lemon trees in the summer months. The wall is draped in the rampant climbing rose, *Rosa filipes* 'Kiftsgate' syn. *Rosa* 'Kiftsgate', with light-green glossy leaves and fragrant clusters of creamy white flowers.

Parterres are useful for outlining tiny beds and giving a sense of structure and formality without overenclosure; they are perfect for small front gardens, which can be difficult to plant up successfully.

PERGOLAS

Pergolas are an excellent use of smaller spaces in compact urban yards and gardens or as 'rooms' in a larger area. They offer shade, privacy and the chance to fill smaller spaces with generous planting.

Pergolas and arbour seats epitomize Mediterranean style and at their simplest can be draped in wisteria, clematis, honeysuckle and ivy, as well as more exotic choices.

Hot pergola

This is the simplest and least expensive of pergolas, making use of a series of wire arches, with a hot planting scheme utilizing eschscholzia, osteospermum, gazania and arctotis (venidium) and arches draped with ipomoea, bougainvillea, *Campsis radicans*, vitis

broad terracing. He and his successors, the Verekers, who bought the house and garden in 1913, developed the grounds over the years. However, when the inventor Otto Overbeck acquired the property in 1928, he introduced exotic and subtropical plants, some of which still survive, like mature *Trachycarpus fortunei* and a huge camphor tree. This style of planting, which has developed ever since, gives the garden its Mediterranean feel, along with its terracing, staircases, gravel paths and glazed pots.

Nick Stewart, head gardener at Overbecks for the last twelve years, has continued to maintain and develop this approach. This is an

and plumbago, and culminating in a massed planting of cannas, with statuary as a focal point. As the canopy of creepers develops, it can be supported with wires stretched between the arches to make a continuous sheltered walkway.

The planting includes:

Annual climbers: morning glories including *Ipomoea purpurea* 'Kniola's Purple-black' and *Ipomoea tricolor* 'Heavenly Blue', and *Thunbergia* Susie Hybrids, mixed black-eyed Susan

Exotic perennials (lifted and overwintered in a conservatory): bougainvillea, cassia, hibiscus and *Plumbago auriculata*

Hardy climbers: the trumpet creeper, *Campsis radicans* 'Flamenco', and *Vitis vinifera* 'Purpurea', an ornamental deciduous vine with brilliant purple foliage all season

There is also underplanting with:

Arctotis hybrida 'Apricot'
Arctotis hybrida 'Cream'
Arctotis fastuosam 'Jaffa Ice'
Agapanthus umbellatus
Ocimum 'Red Rubin' (basil)
Eschsholzia mexicana 'Sun Shades'
Gazania 'Orange'
Gazania 'Sunshine Mixed'
Gazania Talent Series
Gazania 'Torbay Silver'
Osteospermum jucundum var. *compactum*
Osteospermum Nasinga purple
Osteospermum 'Pastel Yellow'
Osteospermum 'Rich Purple'
Osteospermum 'Sparkler'
Osteospermum 'Tresco Purple'
Pelargonium
Portulaca Sundial Series
plus a spring planting of mixed alliums.

Romantic pergola

This is a more romantic pergola, with brick piers, ivy and wisteria, crocosmia and pelargoniums all leading to a focal point. The construction here is much more substantial.

ABOVE **A simple pergola, constructed from low-cost wire arches, is underplanted with osteospermum, gazania and eschsholzia**

BELOW **With a larger budget you can have a brick-built pergola with sturdy piers, to support heavy climbing plants like *Wisteria sinensis***

CHAPTER 4

Hard landscaping and water features

Terraces, steps and stairs evoke formal Italianate gardens with their changing levels and use of statuary and balustrades, while a less formal approach can emulate the Mediterranean cliffside gardens through the use of raised beds and rockeries.

Because Mediterranean-climate plants are adapted to thrive in dry conditions and poor, often chalky, soil, they are especially well suited to planting in steep, sloping, raised or well-drained sites, whether these are pre-existing features of your location or whether they have been created artificially by you. In these well-drained sites you will be able to grow plants which would otherwise be much more difficult to cultivate successfully.

ABOVE This magnificent Italian Garden at Bicton Park Gardens, Devon, south-west England, was established *circa* 1735, reputedly to a design by Versailles landscaper André Le Nôtre. It is one of the very few historical formal gardens surviving in the UK

ABOVE Complementing the historical Italian Garden at Bicton Park in the south-west of England, is this inspiring contemporary Mediterranean Garden, created on a well-drained, south-facing slope and planted with colourful Mediterranean-climate plants, including Australasian species

GARDEN DESIGNS
THE BICTON HOUSE
MEDITERRANEAN GARDEN

The famous eighteenth-century Italian garden at Bicton Park Botanical Gardens, Budleigh Salterton, Devon, in the south-west of England, is one of the few remaining Renaissance-inspired gardens in the United Kingdom. However, the owners, Simon and Valerie Lister, have also developed an interesting contemporary Mediterranean garden at Bicton, which is a sympathetic and interesting addition to the park.

The site flows down a hillside, with a path and steps leading through the centre of it, and the scale is intimate enough to be transferable to a smaller garden. It is planted on a south-facing, well-drained slope.

The planting includes a collection of Mediterranean-style plants, which will provide as much colour as possible throughout the summer, but will also withstand drought during dry periods. Australasian species have also been added.

Some plants are taken in for protection from frost in the winter and there is use made of tender perennials to provide colour for as long as possible in the summer. These plants are the flesh, as it were, on the permanent architectural skeleton provided by phormiums, cordylines, grasses, shrubs and a few trees.

The planting includes the quintessence of the Mediterranean, species of helianthemum, the shrubby evergreen or semi-evergreen, fully hardy and trouble-free rock rose or sun rose, including H. 'Henfield Brilliant', with salmon-red flowers, and H. 'Ben Ledi'.

Evergreen shrubs, cistus species, also confusingly sharing the common name of rock or sun rose, are frost-hardy, including *Cistus x skanbergii* from Greece, with its ¾in (2cm)

ABOVE **This humorous planting at a hotel in Poole, southern England, designed by Kate Elysee, has an area where guests can enjoy drinks on a terrace overlooking a faux Provençal field, with a 'crop' of box and thuja balls interspersed with narrow spires of cypress**

pale-pink flowers with yellow centres. There is a bright underplanting of the white-flowered *Convolvulus cneorum* from southern Europe.

Evergreen shrubby phlomis includes the pink phlomis *Phlomis purpurea* rather than the more usual yellow species *Phlomis fruticosa*, the Jerusalem sage. Perennial, deciduous *Kniphofia* 'Sunningdale Yellow', with long-lasting, slender, primrose-yellow flowers, and a small-flowered evergreen perennial species, red-hot poker *Kniphofia northiae* from South Africa, contrast with a pretty, small-headed, agapanthus, A. 'Lilliput'.

The planting also includes salvia, *Brachyglottis* 'Sunshine', allium, diascia and osteospermum. The unusual apricot-pink spires of

Verbascum 'Pink Petticoats' are used among yellow verbascum cultivars.

Hardy alternatives to this planting:
Substitute fully hardy, though not as free-flowering, Spanish *Convolvulus boissieri* syn. *C. nitidus* for *Convolvulus cneorum*, and potentilla species for cistus.

A TERRACED 'PROVENÇAL' GARDEN
This scheme cleverly suggests a terraced Provençal hillside. A seating area with a yew hedge, *Taxus baccata*, overlooks a naturalistic and aromatic planting that consists of lavender, rosemary and santolina, along with sage and mixed grasses, plus the purple-red *Cordyline*

ABOVE **The Italian Gardens, South Cliff, in Scarborough, north-east England, are nearly 100 years old and are showing their age, but they still have a faded charm, with a pergola overlooking flights of stairs down to a statue of Eros in a formal fountain**

australis 'Purpurea', and *Yucca gloriosa*. The grasses, in softly regimented rows, include *Stipa tenuissima* and *Carex comans* 'Bronze'. *Cupressus sempervirens* 'Pyramidalis' provides a vertical accent.

To the left there is a suggestion of a 'field' with more of the vertical *Cupressus sempervirens* 'Pyramidalis', but this time it has been underplanted with a 'crop' of alternate rows of box balls, *Buxus sempervirens*, and the colour-contrasting spheres of *Thuja orientalis* 'Aurea Nana'.

SCARBOROUGH – THE ITALIAN GARDENS

On a clifftop site in Scarborough, north-east England, the Italian gardens are not as smart as when they were first created, but they have a melancholy charm which is still inspiring.

A decaying pergola heads a sweeping flight of steps where a large *Fatsia japonica* overlooks a hot planting of dahlias and cannas.

The gardens are laid out below in a rectangle with intersecting paths, and there is a large Italianate fountain with a statue of Eros as a central focal point.

63

RHS ROSEMOOR: LADY ANNE'S GARDEN

Lady Anne's Garden, near Torrington, Devon in the south-west of England, has the feeling of the private garden that it once was, created over a period of 40 years by Lady Anne Berry.

The protective walls of the house, built in the 1780s, support acacias and myrtles, while succulents like aloes and tender plants like *Nerium oleander* grow on the veranda. The old kitchen garden, with its sheltering walls, supports a permanent planting of cordylines, phormiums and ginger lilies, and tender plants are bedded out in the summer.

The Old Tennis Court Garden is on a raised, south-west-facing site, and it is the kind of sunny, well-drained area that favours Mediterranean, South African and Australasian plants. Raised beds and a soil enhanced with grit give well-drained conditions so that the plants are grown hard to ripen and survive a northern, cold, wet winter. The beds are given a thick gravel mulch to improve drainage and to retain and reflect heat on the plants. The planting contains a framework of trees, including hardy compact conifers like the dwarf mountain pine, *Pinus mugo*, cultivars like *Pinus mugo* 'Winter Gold', *Pinus mugo* 'Trompenburg' and *Pinus mugo* 'Mops', as well as the dark *Pinus nigra* subsp. *nigra* 'Helga'. *Eucalyptus pauciflora* subsp. *debeuzevillei* is a striking white slash against the dark *Juniperus communis* 'Oblonga Pendula'.

The shrubby Australasian *Ozothamnus rosmarinifolius* 'Silver Jubilee', with silvery grey leaves, has fragrant white flower heads, and

RIGHT The sunny Old Tennis Court Garden at RHS Rosemoor, Devon, in the south-west of England, supports a fine display of plants from Australasia, California, South Africa and the Mediterranean. Raised beds and sharp drainage encourage the plants' extensive root systems

ABOVE In 1959, Lady Anne Berry began to develop the gardens which were to become the nucleus of the RHS Rosemoor in Devon, south-west England. The tender species she loved, like myrtles and acacias, still flourish on the sheltered walls of the original eighteenth-century house

cistus species including C. 'Grayswood Pink', and C. *ladanifer* var. *sulcatus* produce a succession of ephemeral flowers.

Other shrubs include the dramatic and fiercely spiny, fully hardy *Poncirus trifoliata*, which carries large and fragrant 2in (5cm) diameter flowers.

Additional flowers consist of the large, round heads of *Allium cristophii*, hardy *Centaurea bella* from the Caucasus, with its large pink flowerheads, plus tough *Eryngium bourgatii* with attractive dark-green leaves with silver veins and blue or blue-green flowers. The helianthemum

species take in H. 'Ben Fhada' and H. 'Wisley Primrose'. The garden also incorporates hardy *Geranium sanguineum*, the bloody cranesbill from Europe and Turkey, which has magenta flowers, and *Verbena rigida*, which has spires of fragrant purple or magenta flowers.

Aromatic plants include *Thymus serpyllum* 'Russetings' and the French lavender *Lavandula stoechas* subsp. *pedunculata*, which has fewer but taller-growing flower stems than the normal French lavender, while *Artemisia stelleriana* 'Boughton Silver' provides striking silver foliage contrast.

ABOVE This pretty rockery displays house plants outside for the summer or in a conservatory. A small pump operates a water feature which keeps up the humidity if the plants are under glass

RIGHT Your houseplants become stronger and their colours will intensify if you put them outside for the summer months

GIVE YOUR HOUSEPLANTS AN OUTING WITH THE FOLLOWING:

A rockery with a summer (or conservatory) planting of tender exotics

Planting: *Anthurium andraeanum*, spathiphyllum, *Asparagus plumosus*, *Monstera deliciosa*, croton (codiaeum), *dracaena*.

A dressed summer staircase

Planting: *Melocactus peruvianus*, *Melocactus oreas*, *Beaucarnea gracilis*, *Chlorophytum comosum*, *Olea europaea*, *Aeonium arboreum* and *A. arboreum* 'Zwartkop', *Sedum sieboldii*, *Sedum spathulifolium* 'Purpureum'.

A terraced water garden

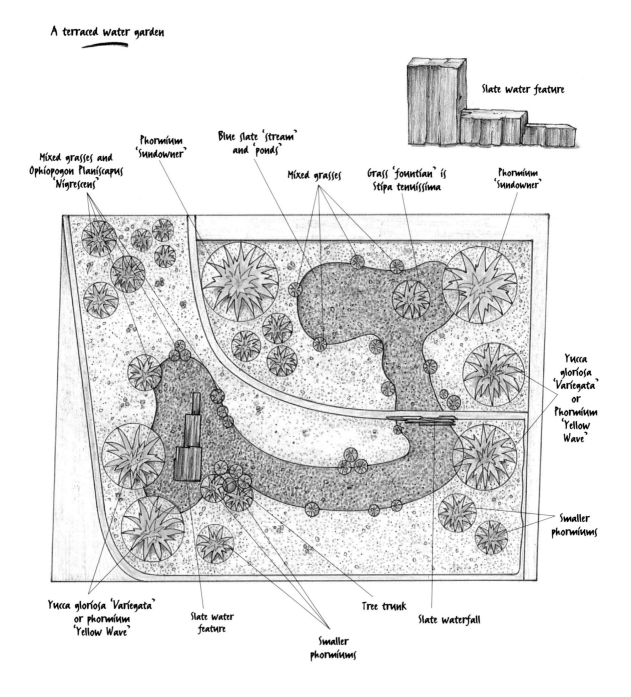

Slate water feature

Phormium 'Sundowner'

Blue slate 'stream' and 'ponds'

Mixed grasses and Ophiopogon Planiscapus 'Nigrescens'

Mixed grasses

Grass 'fountian' is Stipa tenuissima

Phormium 'Sundowner'

Yucca gloriosa 'Variegata' or Phormium 'Yellow Wave'

Smaller phormiums

Yucca gloriosa 'Variegata' or phormium 'Yellow Wave'

Slate water feature

Smaller phormiums

Tree trunk

Slate waterfall

NB: No yuccas were used in the final scheme, seen on the facing page, only phormiums and grasses

ABOVE **After two years the planting has matured into a striking garden. Phormiums were used in a range of sizes and colours and they and the grasses now overhang the edges of the stream and dot the gravel. The only mistake was to plant a *Stipa tenuissima* as a mock fountain in the centre of the top 'pond': it looked great but has self-seeded madly, so this is being replaced with *Astelia* 'Silver Spear' instead**

A TERRACED 'WATER' GARDEN

This bungalow had an uninspiring front garden with terraced lawns and a nondescript tree; it was begging for a complete makeover. The owners liked the idea of a water garden but they did not want the problems associated with installing and maintaining one; so it was decided that the garden should have a mock stream instead.

The grass was stripped off and the site was levelled and lined with a weed-suppressing permeable black membrane. The watercourse, which was faked using blue slate, runs from one upper 'pool' to a second lower one. The top pool has a 'fountain' of the arching grass, *Stipa tenuissima*, which runs on to 'fall' over a blue slate 'waterfall'. From there it 'flows' on to to a second pool that will eventually have a large slate feature, seen in the plan, as a focal point.

However, in every garden design there seems to be some kind of hiccup between the design and the fulfilment. The owners decided to go for a soft planting of grasses and phormiums and to forego the spikier yuccas. The *Stipa tenuissima* looked perfect but unfortunately it also self-seeds so readily that it has been replaced with a well-behaved Astelia 'Silver Spear'. Furthermore, some of the neighbours are still puzzled and continue to ask when the stream is going in! However, as the aerial photograph shows, the design has matured nicely and I think it has a certain appealing impudence about it.

FORMAL 'ISLAMIC' GARDEN

Although still dependent on hard landscaping, the Islamic garden is much more intimate, with smaller pools or water channels. The picture below shows an attractive 'canal' which was part of a complete makeover, where an overgrown shrubbery was replaced with a formal pool, a tiny courtyard with box balls and statue, and a gravelled area with olives and other tender plants in tubs, all overlooked by a wooden bench in a secluded corner.

This plan could be used in its entirety or in separate elements, such as using just the rectangular pool, as seen in the picture below, with the central fountain replaced by a water feature at the end.

This is a very austere look, so to soften the scheme planting ideas can be used from other plans in the book, such as the narrow border and climbers in the courtyard garden illustrated on page 31 or the containers used in the plan on page 37.

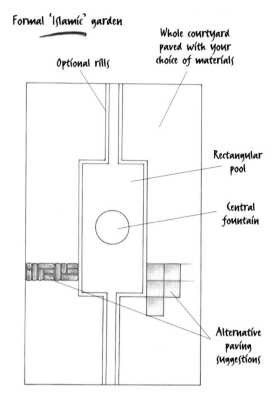

Formal 'Islamic' garden

Optional rills

Whole courtyard paved with your choice of materials

Rectangular pool

Central fountain

Alternative paving suggestions

ABOVE **This is an interpretation of the classical rectangular Islamic pool, which is perfect for any courtyard garden**

ABOVE **The Queen Mother's Garden, Capel Manor College, near London, England, contains this wonderful Italianate pool with balustrading. It has a grand appearance though actually it is in quite an intimate space, so something similar could be introduced into a private garden. This is a high-cost, high-impact approach where the hard landscaping is the major emphasis of the garden**

SHADY COURTYARD

The plan illustrated is based on a garden surrounded by cloisters at the Botanical Garden of Caixa de Girona, Cap Roig, Costa Brava, Spain. This is a perfect example of a courtyard which acts as the central focus to a domestic building (albeit a large one), entirely private and removed from outside access apart from through the house itself, so it epitomizes the courtyard garden as a retreat from the world.

There is a covered arcade through which you can walk all around the outside of the garden, looking in at it through pillars capped with arches. The upper storey of the grand house also looks down and inwards over this courtyard.

The original planting consisted of a gnarled olive, and massed impatiens surrounding a (now dry) central fountain; a small pool with water lilies is flanked by four tiny beds of salvias. The simplified plan has scaled the garden down to domestic proportions, with a specimen tree and a fourfold planting of scarlet pelargoniums surrounded by lavender in little round beds.

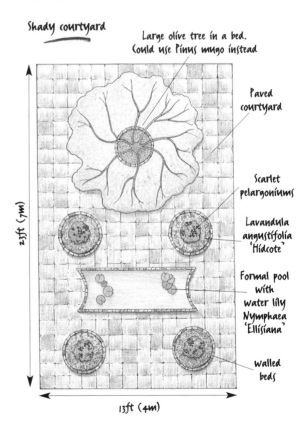

Shady courtyard

Large olive tree in a bed. Could use Pinus mugo instead

Paved courtyard

Scarlet pelargoniums

Lavandula angustifolia 'Hidcote'

Formal pool with water lily Nymphaea 'Ellisiana'

walled beds

23ft (7m)

13ft (4m)

INFORMAL, JUNGLE-LIKE POOL

This informal pool, overlooked by a 'Roman' water-bearer, uses a ready-made pond mould surrounded with a jungle-like monoculture planting of assorted bamboos.

The virtues of bamboos can also be their vices. They are hardy, tolerant and vigorous and will soon make a good display. However, some have insidious habits and they will sneak their way underground quite invisibly until popping up a metre or more away from their parent plants – and so on and on and on...! So be warned that unless you have a known clumping and therefore well-behaved species like *Phyllostachys nigra* and *P. aurea*, be sure to plant them in large, sunken containers where they cannot get out.

Planting details:
Phyllostachys humilis, P. nigra, P. glauca, P. viridiglaucescens, Sasa tessellata, Shibatea humilis, Sasaella masamuena albostriatus, Pleiblastus pygmaeus variegatus, and *Sinarundinaria nitida*

ABOVE In complete contrast to the pictures on pages 70 and 71, this is a more informal, jungly pool, surrounded by bamboo species

BELOW The deep maroon of the wrought-iron furniture on the simple raised decking is picked up by the colours of the phormium in a container and by the heuchera in the gravel beside the clean curved lines of this modern pool

PATIO WITH DECKING, GRASSES AND A CURVING POOL

This small courtyard garden has a number of separate elements, including a raised decking patio edged with colourful pelargoniums, a pretty, honeysuckle-strewn arbour, ornamental grasses, phormiums and mixed containers. The curving pool has clean, modern lines. Consequently, it has a very different feel to the informal bamboo 'jungle' pond.

Although it is a formal and controlled look, it is surprisingly flexible, as you can make dramatic changes with the container planting you introduce. Like the courtyard garden on page 36, it is an ideal sheltered area for bringing out exotic plants like citrus, brugmansia and plumbago for the summer months and then overwintering them in a conservatory.

ABOVE **Steps soften as plants and lichens grow; try edging them with rosemary or lavender for fragrance as you walk by**

Softening architectural features

A freshly constructed flight of stairs or terrace can look very stark; in time they will naturally become softened as plants gain a foothold, twining themselves around balustrades and pillars and creeping across risers. However, it is relatively easy to accelerate this process.

Any crevice in walls or steps can support an abundance of the Mexican daisy, *Erigeron karvinskianus* syn. *E mucronatus*, which originated in Central America but is widely naturalized in Mediterranean-climate areas and in the south-west of England.

In Mediterranean-climate gardens, the walls and edges of beds support trailing succulent mesembryanthemum species that hang in foliage sheets and flower in masses all summer. In a temperate climate, there are hardy species that will create this effect. *Delosperma cooperi* dies down in winter but creates foliage sheets and flowers from the end of spring until the first frost. Ivy species and cultivars (hedera) are vigorous and easy to grow. They will scramble around balustrades and balconies, and trail across steps – but make sure you don't create a trip hazard.

73

CHAPTER 5

Suburban wildernesses

Among the common features of real Mediterranean gardens is their eclectic mix of introduced and naturalized planting. This takes the form of three approaches: the parched 'aridscape' with cacti, succulents and palm trees; the subtropical jungle-like planting, with plenty of bamboo and exotic underplanting; or the looser more natural look, with ornamental grasses and drifts of flowers as a showy alternative to a natural garden.

DESERT AND JUNGLE PLANTING SCHEMES

Many people find it inconceivable that schemes like these can also flourish in temperate gardens, but they can and do; the judicious choice of hardy yuccas, phormiums and palms and cordylines can give a joyously colourful and evergreen year-round framework to a planting enlivened with less hardy aloes and agaves. New Zealand phormiums originate in temperate areas, so will live and grow happily down to temperatures of 10°F (−12°C). The numerous cultivars have been bred to give an array of colour, from variegated white and green, to various pinks, reds and bronzes, to the black 'Platt's Black' and miniature 'Jack Spratt'.

The frost-hardy banana *Musa basjoo* is root-hardy in all regions and will produce large soft leaves like elephant ears to tower at the back of borders or in the middle of island beds.

This suckering plant will throw up several stems and produce a nice little grove for you. It will reach 15ft (4.5m) in height and a spread of 12ft (3.6m) in habitat, but a year's growth will give you a 6½ft (2m) tall plant with leaves up to 10ft (3m) long, and, though the wind may give them a battering, there are always new and pristine replacements until the frosts arrive.

At the nursery, we have numerous exotic spots, including cactus rockeries, cactus and succulent beds, and areas with palms, cordylines, tree ferns, bamboo and banana. We have been developing the nursery gardens over the last twelve years or so, and what we

EXTEND YOUR PLANTING

If you are keen and have a spirit of adventure, you can experiment with all sorts of unlikely plants. To extend the range of plants you can grow, try the following:
1. run heating cables through outside beds to extend the planting
2. wrap your plants up in the winter
3. keep a heated conservatory – copy Louis XIV and have an orangery where your delicate plants can be overwintered. This is the origin of the Versailles tub, which was designed to be wheeled in and out.

ABOVE Raised, well-drained beds at our nursery, like the one in the background, support a mixture of cacti and succulents which have endured wet and cold winters with temperatures down to 14°F (−10°C). In the foreground, half-hardy plants enjoy their summer outing

have now are the plants that have survived for many years at temperatures of 14°F (−10°C) and lower with some prolonged wet and cold winters and strong gales. Where we live we are surrounded by drained marshland, so we have a high water table and damp, fertile soil.

How have we done it? Ours is a sheltered site, with trees and hedges all around. We use raised beds to assist with drainage and make full use of south-facing borders and warm walls. We do not give anything winter protection, as we feel we need to try everything out.

The cactus and succulent rockery is about six years old, and we have plenty of flowering opuntias and aloes (including *Aloe striatula*), an underplanting of globular cacti like echinocereus and chamaecereus, trailing

succulents (including lots of *Delosperma cooperi*), and all sorts of other succulents, (including yuccas, crassulas and sedums).

A second cactus bed along a south-facing wall has opuntias again, including low-growing *Opuntia compressa*, which is a mass of yellow flowers in the summer. Gazanias self-seed freely under blue *Agave americana* and thread through the smaller cacti and *Aloe aristata*. A mature branching *Cordyline australis* has reached bedroom-window height and flowers every year; self-set cordyline seedlings are a constant menace!

We have a 15ft (4.5m) tall bamboo hedge of mixed *Phyllostachys nigra* and *P. aurea*, which shelters *Brahea armata*, *Butia capitata* and dwarf *Trachycarpus wagnerianus*. Lots of

ABOVE **If you look closely at the rock on the left, you can see an alert meerkat guarding his suitably exotic surroundings**

cordylines grow and flower. *Dicksonia antarctica* and a big clump of *Musa basjoo* grow among mixed phormiums, some of which are 10ft (3m) tall.

GARDEN DESIGNS
AN ARIDSCAPE PLANTING

This 'aridscape' rockery, shown above and on the left, uses desert planting with hardy and half-

LEFT **Tim Miles, head gardener at the Cotswold Wildlife Park, Burford, west England, has used an imaginative mix of hardy and half-hardy plants, including cacti, succulents, palms and gazanias to landscape the surroundings of the meerkat enclosure, also shown above**

ABOVE **For several years this sunny sandstone cliff face in the south-east of England has been used as a 'hanging garden' for an assortment of cacti, succulents and other drought-resistant plants that grow and flower happily in free-draining crevices**

hardy plants. This exciting scheme at the Cotswold Wildlife Park in Burford, in the west of England is actually the surrounds to the meerkat enclosure; the rockery is formed as cladding of the indoor quarters and landscaped with an interesting mix of planting, much of which is year round. Another impressive innovation is the use of underground heating cables to extend the planting.

There is an eclectic planting with: *Butia capitata, Cordyline australis, Aeonium arboreum, Aloe arborescens, Carpobrutus edulis, Echeveria glauca, Cereus peruvianus* var. *monstrosus, Oreocereus celsianus* with other mixed cacti and succulents including aeoniums, agaves, aloes, crassulas, cleistocactus, dasylirion, echeverias and yuccas, plus terrestrial bromeliads and gazanias.

A SUSSEX CACTUS CLIFF

This cliff face (pictured above) in East Grinstead in the south-east of England, is a 20ft (6.1m) high sandstone cliff which has been planted with an assortment of cacti and succulents in a damp cement and compost mix that has literally been stuck in place.

ABOVE The warm tones and softly weeping outlines of the phormiums soften the otherwise stark paving, and they can be trimmed back when they become overgrown. Gravel complements the plants and prevents lots of weeds from growing through

EXOTIC PLANTING SCHEME AT THE BASE OF A WALL, STEPS AND RAISED PATIO

This is a simple scheme consisting of a band of colourful phormiums along the pathway and an architectural planting of palms, with *Trachycarpus fortunei* underplanted with the shrubbier *Chamaerops humilis*.

A massed planting of Phormiums is used, including *Phormium* 'Apricot Queen', which is an outstanding dwarf form that makes a low weeping structure of about 30 x 30in (76 x 76cm). It has beautiful cream leaves that are flushed apricot when young, maturing to a pale creamy yellow with green and bronze margins. *Phormium* 'Rainbow Queen' is also included. This is an upright form with drooping tips. It grows to 3–5ft (91cm–1.5m) high, and has dramatic tones with bronze/green foliage and pink-red margins. In addition, the vigorous *Phormium* 'Yellow Wave' has been planted. This also has a drooping habit, and it reaches a height of 3ft (91cm). Its green leaves develop strong pale-yellow variegation after the first few inches of growth.

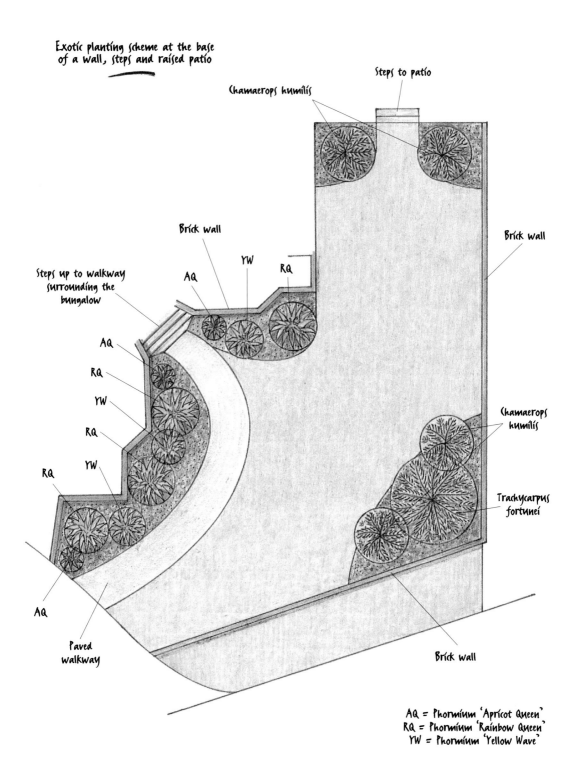

Exotic planting scheme at the base
of a wall, steps and raised patio

Steps to patio

Chamaerops humilis

Brick wall

Brick wall

Steps up to walkway
surrounding the
bungalow

YW

AQ

RQ

AQ

RQ

YW

RQ

RQ

YW

Chamaerops
humilis

Trachycarpus
fortunei

AQ

Paved
walkway

Brick wall

AQ = Phormium 'Apricot Queen'
RQ = Phormium 'Rainbow Queen'
YW = Phormium 'Yellow Wave'

ABOVE This natural-looking 'Californian wild meadow', planted between grape vines, was actually created for the 2003 Chelsea Flower Show in London, England, to illustrate the organic approach to viniculture used at the Bonterra Organic Wine Garden in the USA

MEADOWS AND GRASSLANDS

Although a strong element of Mediterranean-style gardening is formality, an alternative approach is to use Mediterranean-climate flowering plants with ornamental grasses to create an exotic-wild-flower-meadow effect.

GARDEN DESIGNS

BONTERRA ORGANIC WINE GARDEN

At the 2003 Chelsea Flower Show in London, England, the Bonterra Organic Wine Garden illustrated the vineyard's use of cover crops like clover, vetch, oats, peas and wildflowers planted between the rows of vines to promote soil health and to encourage beneficial insects. They use mixes like the native annuals, including the self-seeding Californian poppy, *Eschscholzia californica*, the self-seeding nectar-rich poached-egg flower, *Limnanthes douglasii*, which grows to 6in (15cm) in height and spread and is attractive to bees and hoverflies, the hardy perennial birdsfoot trefoil, *Lotus corniculatus*, with its pealike yellow flowers, the northern temperate cornflower, hardy annual *Centaurea cyanus* which grows to 8–32in (20–81cm) tall with a spread of 6in (15cm), the much-loved common field poppy, *Papaver rhoeas,* and the red clover, *Trifolium pratense.*

ABOVE Half-hardy annuals create a carpet of flowers in one season and can be grown from seeds or brought in as small plants

ABOVE **A meadow of ornamental grasses and perennial flowers is a really colourful and easy-to-care-for feature, as it smothers weed growth, and the only maintenance it requires is trimming dead growth each spring and cutting back plant 'bullies'**

Try *Eschscholzia californica* mixed with South African tender perennials like gazania and osteospermum for a lavish, colourful carpet.

For a longer-lasting approach you could have a planting of long-flowering perennials and ornamental grasses on their own or in combination for year-round colour and interest.

MEADOW OF PERENNIAL FLOWERS AND ORNAMENTAL GRASSES

The plot on the facing page is irregularly shaped; the diagonal edge is 15ft (4.6m) long, while the short edge is 3ft (91cm) across and the longer edge is 8ft (2.4m).

The illustrated scheme uses taller-growing and showy grasses. One of the best is the 3ft (91cm) tall *Phalaris arundinacea* var. *picta*, which has the common name of 'gardener's garters'. It is one of the most striking of the white-and-green-striped grasses. Other musts are the variegated miscanthus, including *Miscanthus sinensis* 'Cosmopolitan', a dramatic large plant which can grow to a height of 8ft

(2.4m) and has wide, white-margined leaves that measure up to 2in (5cm) wide. Slightly smaller selections, at 5ft (1.5m) high, are *M. sinensis* 'Morning Light' and *Miscanthus sinensis* 'Zebrinus'. These grasses are combined with *Achillea filipendulina* 'Cloth Of Gold', and *A. millefolium* 'Summer Pastels', scarlet *Geum chiloense* 'Mrs J. Bradshaw', and massed crocosmias.

Other grasses which you could consider include the architectural stipas, or giant feather grasses, and the yellow splash of *Milium effusum* 'Aureum', also known as 'Bowles's golden grass', while eryngium, *Penstemon* 'Juggler', *Lobelia cardinalis* 'Queen Victoria', kniphofia and echinops also combine well. You can try varying the planting plan from discrete blocks to 'ribbons' that thread sinuously through the completed scheme. There is scope, too, for a much lower planting plan, with smaller grasses, intermingling with flowers.

This scheme looks good almost all year round, with both seed heads and old growth

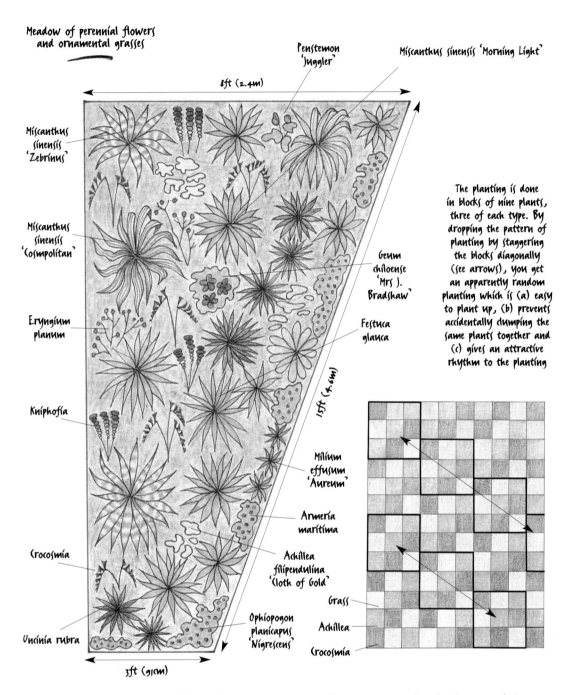

Meadow of perennial flowers and ornamental grasses

8ft (2.4m)

Penstemon 'Juggler'

Miscanthus sinensis 'Morning Light'

Miscanthus sinensis 'Zebrinus'

Miscanthus sinensis 'Cosmpolitan'

Geum chiloense 'Mrs J. Bradshaw'

Eryngium planum

Festuca glauca

15ft (4.6m)

The planting is done in blocks of nine plants, three of each type. By dropping the pattern of planting by staggering the blocks diagonally (see arrows), you get an apparently random planting which is (a) easy to plant up, (b) prevents accidentally clumping the same plants together and (c) gives an attractive rhythm to the planting

Kniphofia

Milium effusum 'Aureum'

Crocosmia

Armeria maritima

Achillea filipendulina 'Cloth of Gold'

Uncinia rubra

Ophiopogon planicapus 'Nigrescens'

Grass

Achillea

Crocosmia

3ft (91cm)

providing an austere and sombre winter structure that is particularly effective when touched by frost. However, it does need to be cut away in the early spring, so if you don't want a hiatus while you wait for the new growth to appear, a lavish planting of dramatic spring bulbs – drifts of pure white narcissi, for example, showy black tulips like 'Queen of the Night' or the large round heads of alliums – will fill the gap for you.

83

CHAPTER 6

Bed and border exotics

The Mediterranean-style border is epitomized by bright colour, which gives the impression of heat and brilliant light, even when the weather in cooler climes is dull and grey.

This alternative to the traditional herbaceous or mixed borders uses exciting schemes, with palms, phormiums, yuccas and bananas for height and 'hot' combinations of exotic flowers and foliage, both hardy and half-hardy, together with flowers such as cannas, echiums, echinops, osteospermum and gazanias.

This isn't a style that uses pastel-themed borders or has a gentle cottage-garden look, hinting at roses round the door and a chocolate-box garden overflowing with hollyhocks and lupins; this is a bold, confrontational approach, where you want eye-dazzling colour to provide that sun-soaked feel.

In this chapter you will find lots of pictures of Mediterranean-style beds in temperate gardens, taken in spring and autumn (fall), which demonstrate numerous inspirational schemes, including the use of architecturals like bananas and palms as focal planting.

Although some of the planting uses Mediterranean-climate plants, there is also space for plants that simply provide the right look: this includes bold foliage and brilliant colours, plus a feeling of generosity and abundance. Of course, all of the schemes can be adapted to suit your particular site and rearranged to taste.

Gallery of planting schemes

Trachycarpus fortunei (below left); *Trachycarpus fortunei* with *Cordyline australis* (left), and *Yucca gloriosa* 'Variegata' (right) all make dramatic centrepieces.

Arundo donax, the giant Mediterranean reed, is a showy and tall-growing grass (1). It is a wonderful filler that will grow quickly while you wait for more slow-growing exotics to mature; for a more flickering effect, it is also available as *Arundo donax* 'Variegata'. The plain grass acts as a good contrast to the variegated spiky *Yucca gloriosa* 'Variegata' (2), the pelargonium with its showy leaves (3) and also the bright-red phormium cultivar (4).

This is an altogether edgier planting, with another hardy palm *Chamaerops humilis* (1) and a grouping of *Yucca gloriosa* 'Variegata' (2), again with the variegated pelargonium (3) and the soft leaves and drooping flower spikes of the hostas (4).

Musa basjoo, the hardy banana, is a very flashy herbaceous centrepiece; these plants are root-hardy, and the stem will often survive to give you a head start for the following season. If you have space, you can lift them for the winter; otherwise you can preserve the trunk by wrapping it in hessian for the winter in colder areas. Here, *Musa sp.* (banana) combines with colourful impatiens to turn an ordinary bedding display into something striking.

Pelargonium hybrids (bedding geraniums) are great choices for bright colour, prolific flower and relative drought resistance, and they often have the added benefit of foliage interest.

Try pelargoniums (1) with red cordyline (2) and the half-hardy shrub *Ricinus communis* (3) and (4), grown as an annual, with architectural foliage leaves (Ricinus is a highly toxic plant, though, especially the seeds, so use with care). Alternatively, try them with *Solenostemon scutellarioides* (left), commonly known as coleus or flame nettle, as a great foliage backdrop with splashes of bright colour. Even on its own, coleus (bottom left) can act as a blaze of trouble-free colour.

Astelia chathamica 'Silver Spear' grows 4ft (1.2m) high to 6ft (1.8m) across and is from New Zealand. It is another architectural focal point, and here subtly contrasts with impatiens.

Look for the South American annuals, cleome and nicotiana. *Cleome hassleriana* syn. *C. spinosa* (spider flower) (1) is a much underrated and exotic half-hardy annual, reaching 5ft (1.5m) tall. Combined with *Nicotiana sylvestris*, which reaches the same height, it makes a breathtaking border with an underplanting of Southern European annual *Iberis umbellata*, (candytuft). It is also good with the sword-like foliage and even taller flower spikes of cannas and the good-tempered impatiens (busy lizzie) as underplanting – these will flower more or less anywhere, in shade or sun, and are often seen in Mediterranean gardens. In a looser planting it combines well with the stripy *Canna* 'Tropicanna' (2) and the daisy-like heads of cosmos (3).

In this kind of border you can go for the most dramatic colour combinations, along with textural variations. You can be subtle – severe box (above) is enlivened with the red splash of salvia – or vivid, where bright-yellow *Lysimachia punctata* contrasts with the red of geum and the white tracery of heuchera flowers (right). You can also be textural, where the yellow spikes of *Lysimachia punctata* contrast with the flat yellow heads of *Achillea filipendula* 'Cloth of Gold' and spires of lavender and echinops buds (far right), or contrasting, where the maroon-black foliage of *Dahlia* 'Yellow Hammer' is massed with the yellow foliage of *Solenostemon scutellarioides* (bottom).

ABOVE **Agastache**

ABOVE **Filmy purple *Verbena bonariensis***

ABOVE ***Angelica gigas* with agastache**

BELOW ***Acanthus spinosus* and echinops**

Spikes, spires and globes are also great value. The dramatic dark heads of *Angelica gigas* combine well with the paler spires of *Agastache foeniculum*, and there are good colour contrasts with verbascum, verbena, hosta and phormium, Mediterranean *Acanthus spinosus* and echinops, *Onopordum acanthium*, and the pink umbels of *Eupatorium purpureum*.

LEFT **This display includes *Verbascum olympicum* (1), hostas (2), and phormium (3)**

ABOVE **The very tall, branching, architectural plant is *Onopordum acanthium***

RIGHT **The spiky phormium in the foreground is a good contrast to the soft pink umbels of *Eupatorium purpureum* at the back on the left**

CHAPTER 7

Container planting

You may only have the tiniest of areas in which to garden – a small yard or perhaps just the space around the entrance to your house or flat. Alternatively, you may want to brighten up an otherwise drab area of paving and decking, where there is no possibility of planting in the ground. If so, your garden can be largely or wholly container-based. Choosing succulents will give almost maintenance-free containers, as the plants will manage happily on natural rainfall, except for in the driest of summers. You could also use mixed planting to create a medley of changing displays, group individual plants together in pots, or even make a focal point out of particularly eye-catching empty pots.

For all containers, choose a loam-based compost, like a John Innes mixture, and select the one with the highest nutrient content like JI3 or the equivalent. Put a good layer of drainage material in the bottom of the pot. Traditionally pebbles or pieces of broken clay pots are used for this, but you can use pieces of polystyrene packing material instead, as this gives you a lightweight container that you can easily move around. This is particularly useful when you want to use an assortment of displays, because you can move a fresh pot into place as soon as others are past their best.

Gallery of planting schemes

CONTAINER-BASED GARDENS

Containers of *Agave americana* 'Variegata' (1),
a warty aloe (2), a standard bay (3) and frosty-
coloured echeverias (4) brighten up the area
around a front door. Affordable ceramics come
in a variety of shades and can be chosen to
harmonize with your planting arrangement.

Agave americana 'Variegata' (3) again,
this time grouped with *Aeonium arboreum*
(2) and *Aeonium arboreum* 'Zwartkop' (1),
along with a rather downcast Buddha,
add interest to an otherwise dull corner.

Cordyline australis 'Purple Tower' (1) combines with the delicate pink of Echeveria 'Perle von Nurnberg' (2) in a container against a hedera-covered wall (3); there is also a clever continuation of outside/inside and vice versa in the pots of echeverias (4) and Crassula ovata (5) in the window.

Adding containers lends versatility to your garden, as you can easily change your displays, either by rearranging or substituting the pots and bowls. Simple containers of succulents like Aeonium arboreum 'Zwartkop' (1) and the large-leaved cultivar Aeonium arboreum (3) combine sympathetically with slightly more demanding containers of variegated grasses like Acorus gramineus 'Variegatus' (4) and Ophiopogon planiscapus 'Nigrescens' (2).

Often in life, less is more, as with these simple chimney pots, which are planted to overflowing with vivid deep-red pelargoniums and enlivened with a surprising flash of lilac. Although they need more watering than succulent planters, pelargoniums will manage on far less water and feed than some of the thirstier summer bedders.

Curiosities like *Juncus effusus f. spriralis*, the twisted rush, need more water but are worth it for their eccentricity.

At its most severe, box (*Buxus sempervirens*) in containers can lend an austere elegance to stairs and entrances.

MIXED CONTAINERS

Add eye-dazzling mixed containers to any
garden; they will give value until the frost comes.
You can mix summer flowers with spiky palms
and other architectural plants for an effective mix
of colour and shape, like this snippet of
Chamaerops humilis with lampranthus and
pelargoniums (below left), *Chamaerops humilis*
with a mass of petunias and ivy-leaved
pelargoniums (right), and *Trachycarpus fortunei*
with a mass of red pelargoniums (below right).

Yellow *Bidens ferulifolia*
again, this time in
combination with a dark
contrast of hedera.

Yellow *Bidens
ferulifolia* is
another reliable
sun-lover from
South America
and Mexico to
give a hot flash
of colour. In the
container
pictured on the
right it is planted
in combination
with ivy-leaved
pelargoniums,
petunias and
felicia.

You can brighten the darkest corner with a burst of summer colour, as with this hedera and pelargonium group, planted in a hanging basket (right). However, tthe plant of choice for a really dark corner is impatiens, which will flower everywhere.

Pelargoniums are also used here to blaze from a dark corner – once this Virginia creeper becomes established and covers the pot, the effect will be stunning.

In this scheme, clipped box and conifers are set off by a riot of summer bedding; you can extend the look by planting winter-flowering pansies to follow on.

GOING SOLO

Some of the most dramatic containers, though, are the monoculture ones, where a group of a single species, or a single plant, makes a proud statement of its own. Some of the showiest are the higher-maintenance options, like the ivy-leaved pelargonium, marguerites, osteospermum (left and bottom right), agapanthus (bottom left) and the wonderful angels' trumpets or brugmansia – but they are certainly worth the effort. Foliage choices like box and phormium are an effective contrast to brighter planting, but other succulents and true cacti are winners in terms of ease of care, such as the colourful rosettes of echeverias (middle top), the weird swollen *Pachypodium lamerei* (middle bottom), the profusely flowering *Lampranthus roseus*, and cacti such as *Echinocactus grusonii*, spitefully named 'mother-in-law's cushion' or this spiky opuntia species, whose yellow flowers are followed by swollen purple fruits (top right).

Simplest of all is planting just the empty pots! From the ultra-modern to the Moroccan, to the cool Egyptian, through classical, and ending with the apparent ethnic or rustic discards, pots on their own can be as effective as any amount of planting, acting as focal points, breaking up dark areas and generally adding interest to any plan.

SECTION 3

CHAPTER 8
Style on a budget
102

Style on a budget

We could all have the perfect house and garden of our dreams if only we possessed the budget. This section is intended to help the many people who have inspiration and ambition and not enough money to put their ideas into practice.

TOPIARY

Popular since Roman times and a staple of the formal garden throughout garden history, topiary is the cliché of the chic hotel entrance and of every swish doorway in smart parts of the city. However, it is a bit like bonsai: it takes immense

ABOVE **Massed topiary in a myriad of shapes at the Funchal Botanical Garden in Madeira**

ABOVE **You can buy or make wire formers, like this spiral, to help you to train your topiary. Clip the plant to the shape as it grows**

'Suffruticosa', an ideal, compact, slow-growing dwarf, reaching a height of 3ft (91cm) and a spread of 5ft (1.5m), perfect for small hedges around flower beds or herb beds. Yew (*Taxus baccata*) is another popular choice, as is the bushy evergreen honeysuckle *Lonicera nitida*. The common hornbeam (*Carpinus betulus*), bay (*Laurus nobilis*), holly (*ilex*) species and privet (*Ligustrum ovalifolium*) are also used.

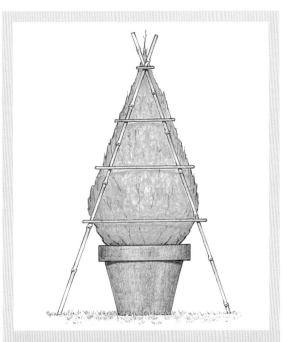

patience to grow from scratch and is expensive to buy ready-made. By far the cheapest approach is to grow your own. For maximum flexibility, keep your plants in pots and they can be moved around to ring the changes – and you can take them with you if you move house.

The plant of preference in a Mediterranean climate is *Cupressus sempervirens*, the Italian or Mediterranean Cyprus, but in temperate areas small-leaved evergreens with a dense growth and the ability to recover rapidly and easily from clipping are better for formal topiary. Therefore, the plants of choice include the common box, *Buxus sempervirens*, which has a height and spread of 15ft (4.5m) (though there are growing disease problems with this species), or the slower-growing *Buxus sempervirens*

For a simple cone, use canes and wire to give you the guide shape to cut to; for more complex shapes you can make or buy metal frames – the more robust the better – and keep the plant clipped to the framework. Clip plants in the growing season at four-to-six-weekly intervals if you want a perfect manicure, twice a year if you can tolerate a shaggier look.

Propagate box, bay, honeysuckle, privet and yew by taking semi-ripe cuttings in the summer, using shoots that have hardened and thickened, and hornbeam by green-wood cuttings in summer, using fresh new shoots.

LEFT **A good low-cost alternative to topiary is quick-growing ivy, which will soon clothe any structure in an evergreen overcoat**

a dense overcoat of matt green or variegated green and white or green and yellow leaves. You can buy a large plant and carefully weave it over the structure you want to use, or buy several smaller plants and tuck them into place as they grow. You can clip the plants at any time to keep the shape you want.

For a simple pillar with a ball on top, you can train ivy up a pole and attach two hanging baskets wired together at the top for the sphere. Ivy can scuttle up the pole and through the wires and then be clipped to shape; you can also construct a form with chicken wire, buy topiary shapes or use ready-made supports like bird tables. Sandwiching a layer of moss between two layers of wire speeds up the growth.

HARD LANDSCAPING

If you don't mind using artificial materials, there is a plethora of stone substitutes you can buy at your local DIY store or garden centre. You can purchase very natural-looking textured material as slabs and in bigger pieces for paving large areas, sections of smaller cobbles and pavers wired together to lay almost carpet-like squares, plus circles and other ready-made shapes.

If you have to have the real thing, but also have a strict budget, then try using expensive materials sparingly, like a few special paving slabs in gravel to extend the area covered.

INSTANT TOPIARY

While your own topiary grows – or while you accumulate the money for it – you can try this instant topiary instead.

The hedera species are a great choice for instant topiary because ivy is self-clinging and grows rapidly, so it will cover any structure with

RIGHT **If you are on a tight budget you can still get a stylish feel by using a few special pieces of paving set into cheaper gravel**

LEFT **Warm terracotta paving evokes a Mediterranean feel, and it is given extra interest by the mix of size and direction in its layout**

Alternatively, you could go completely modern and minimalist with Mediterranean blue-glass chippings, contrasted with arrangements of other materials to surround a smart deck.

Nothing evokes the Mediterranean more than the warm terracotta tones of its paving; you can add immediate warmth to your hard landscaping by using warm earth tones. You can also add cheaper materials like gravel and pebbles to eke out expensive materials, or use lower-cost materials like pavers then concentrate on colour and pattern to add flair.

Stones and slabs in gravel provide a cheap yet stylish look, while slate makes an exciting surface and can be found in a range of grey, blue, purple and green shades.

ABOVE **This mixture of coloured-glass chippings and contrasting hard materials in a severely geometrical layout has a contemporary look**

BELOW **This patio uses a hard landscaping of pavers, complemented by a child-friendly water feature splashing onto cobbles**

Softening and ageing hard landscaping

Part of the magic of the romantic, Italianate garden is the feeling of slightly decayed grandeur, a semi-ruined charm, where weather-stained hard landscaping is softened with moss and lichen, and where ivy and climbers scramble over the walls.

There are some quick cheats to accelerate this softening and ageing process. If you are lucky enough to have a stone balustrade, or other wooden or metal railing, you can soften it with climbing and trailing plants, such as hederas and evergreen honeysuckles. Stair risers can support erigeron or *Soleirolia soleirolii*, syn. *Helxine soleirolii* ('Baby's Tears', or 'Mind Your Own Business'), which will grow in the smallest pocket of soil. You can also train hedera alongside and across the back of each step. However, you must be careful to ensure that the stairs are safe for their primary purpose.

LEFT **A bronze mermaid, by Maria Llimona, rises from a sea of ivy in the Santa Clotilde Botanical Garden, Costa Brava, Spain**

BELOW **Ivy smothers the stair risers of the romantic Italianate staircases, also at the Santa Clotilde Botanical Garden in Spain**

Adding gravel beds to lawns can be a problem if the gravel is not to be mixed up with the mower blades and grass is not to invade the gravel. The diagrams show some solutions to this perennial irritation.

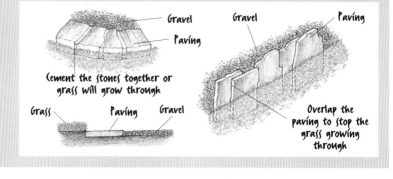

Gravel / Gravel / Paving

Paving

Cement the stones together or grass will grow through

Grass / Paving / Gravel

Overlap the paving to stop the grass growing through

HOW TO AGE AND DISTRESS STAIRS AND STATUES USING YOGHURT

Although time will solve everything, you probably don't want to wait for that pristine, freshly purchased look to fade. You could try buying older pieces instead. After houses are demolished, all sorts of interesting pieces end up in reclamation yards, where you might find just the thing you want. Be warned, though, that other people have the same idea, and prices have risen steeply as a result. You could also try house-clearance auctions or garage and car boot sales. Alternatively, if you can afford to buy new, some garden statue suppliers will sell pieces with a pre-aged look.

However, some of us are going to buy 'classical' statuary which is neither old nor real stone, so, if you have to use newly bought pieces, this yoghurt trick is ideal. You must use a live plain yoghurt and add water until you get a creamy consistency that can be poured or painted onto paving slabs, statues, balustrades and other stonework. The yoghurt feeds the natural organisms, like mosses and lichens, that grow and cover the surface, so the coating will appear much more quickly.

If your statue is porous, you can stir garden soil into water to make a thick suspension that can then be painted on and takes that fresh-from-the-garden-centre look away. (This is also a useful tip if you hang new bird boxes in trees – the birds

ABOVE Age an everyday piece by mixing live yoghurt to a creamy consistency with water and pouring or painting it on your statue

are not so alarmed and become accustomed to them very quickly.) Pond water is also a rich source of micro-organisms and will provide instant discolouration to a porous surface.

OTHER STATUES AND FOCAL POINTS

If you don't like pastiche of classical pieces, choose a modern focal point instead. Driftwood, twisted branches and roots make great conversation pieces and are available at every price, from those you find yourself that cost you nothing, to purchases of natural driftwood

RIGHT Natural Driftwood Sculptures supply water-worn reminders of the Canadian logging industry that make effective focal points

ABOVE Heather Jansch has created this sculpture using cork and deadwood. It stands in the Mediterranean area in the Warm Temperate Biome at the Eden Project, Cornwall, south-west England

LEFT Dovecotes, like this one from the Probus Gardens in Cornwall, south-west England, make pretty centrepieces for any garden

COLOUR AND BACKDROPS

The blue-paint revolution has alienated a lot of people, but there is still a case for paint in the garden. Pale or pastel colour-washed walls and fences provide an instant Mediterranean feel and create a bright space for outdoor living while also giving plants extra reflected light for maximum growth. Sheds and garage walls can give a brilliant backdrop for climbing plants and/or arrangements of pots and containers.

We don't all have the walled gardens of our dreams. Often, a backdrop is a pre-existing hedge, which, when well clipped, makes a good canvas for your other planting. If you can't afford a new fence, or if the fence you have is in good condition but not very attractive, use

rescued from old logging mills in Canada. If you are artistic, you may be able to create something from metal or wood – or go to evening classes to learn how. Dovecotes, sundials and armillary spheres are also interesting talking points. Local artists may be able to offer fascinating pieces; speak to art students if you are on a tight budget.

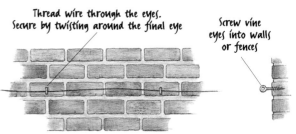

Thread wire through the eyes. Secure by twisting around the final eye

Screw vine eyes into walls or fences

ABOVE Train your plants by fastening them to the wire; use garden twine or thread the stems through to get them started if they are self-clinging

vine eyes and wires trained across it so that you can clothe it with a billowing mass of evergreen foliage and flowering climbers. Trellis is another option. For a non-foliage backcloth, try attaching a bamboo or brushwood screen to give a more interesting background.

TILES
Tiles are colourful and evocative of hot climates. Although Spanish, South American and Moroccan tiles can be sealed against damp to protect them from frost, it is far better to search out lookalikes, such as frost-proof Italian tiles.

RILLS
The Moorish influence in southern Spain is reflected in the tiny rills which run in paving, along the tops of walls, down stairways and suchlike. They are very easy to replicate with the use of roof tiles cemented together and overlapping to create a fall. Otherwise you can line a narrow channel with pond liner and edge it with overlapping flat tiles, as illustrated below.

ABOVE **A colourful tiled panel like this, made up of frost-proof tiles, is an ideal focal point for a small walled garden**

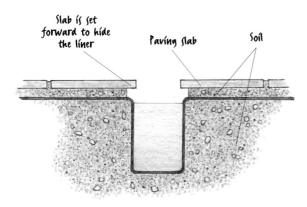

ABOVE **Cut out a narrow channel to form the rill and line it with pond liner. The pond liner overlaps the edge of the rill. Layers of soil secure the liner in place. A paving slab is laid over the soil**

RIGHT **The classic rill is a formal geometrical feature that is typical of Islamic gardens, either on its own or leading into a larger water feature**

Mosaics

This is another opportunity to unleash the artist in you, by making your own mosaic and/or cobble patterns for walls and paving. It is not difficult but it is time-consuming, so you need patience and some uninterrupted stretches of time for this.

Pebble mosaics can be amusing and interesting and you can also embed all sorts of mementos of your own in quick-setting cement, such as seashells or pottery with sentimental value. You can involve your children in selecting and arranging pieces, though you will need to do the actual laying, as cement is an irritant. Do wear gloves to protect your hands.

There are two techniques for laying mosaic: direct and indirect.

DIRECT METHOD

This is a quick and easy way of making mosaic pieces to cement into a wall or into a patio between normal paving slabs, or alternatively for creating a decorative garden feature.

It has the advantage that you can see exactly what you are doing and how the design is progressing. A large project, though, can be hard on your knees, and you will need good weather. The project is subdivided by formers, which are either card or thin wooden shapes to contain the mosaic sections, and the design is then built up piece by piece in units of one square yard (one square metre).

For a single paving slab, lay out your design on a piece of paper or card the same size and shape as your slab – draw round your slab if it is an irregular shape. You can use pebbles, glass beads, slate and cobbles to construct your pattern.

Paint the slab with PVA glue to seal it. Outline the shape with a cardboard strip and fix it in place with strong tape; this will be the container and former for your design. Fill the former with quick-setting cement and add your design – quickly!

ABOVE Mrs Dorrien-Smith, co-owner of the Abbey Gardens, Tresco, Isles of Scilly, created this grotto there, with its elaborate seashell mosaics

ABOVE Informal direct-method paths are a big feature of parks and gardens all over the Mediterranean, like this example in Spain

ABOVE **Try your design, using pebbles, glass beads and pieces of slate, on a piece of card the size and shape of your finished slab**

ABOVE **Use a strip of cardboard to divide the slab into smaller sections, pour in quick-setting cement, and lay your mosaic pieces**

INDIRECT METHOD

The direct method is not a good technique for a mosaic pavement or patio that will need to stand heavy wear and tear. In this case you would need to use the indirect method, which is ideal for large projects that need to be perfectly flat.

You will need to create a mould around a strong, flat board, using timber lengths that are about 3–3½in (8–9cm) deep at right angles to the board.

Hold them firmly in place with tape and wooden blocks or bricks around the edges. Place the pebbles upside down in a bed of sand then work sand in around them. Spray the sand and pebbles with water then pour in a layer of a non-shrinking cement-based grout, and vibrate to remove air bubbles. After two hours or so the grout will have set enough to add the concrete. Use a 3:2:1 mix of ⅜in (10mm) aggregate,

sand and cement with the least possible water. Fill the mould, vibrating it again to remove air bubbles. Cover with polythene and after 24 to 48 hours remove the mould. Turn the slab over and hose the sand off. For full strength, wrap the slab in polythene and cure it for four weeks. The end result is very strong; several pieces can be constructed then joined together in situ.

ABOVE **Your design can be really personal. This one uses the family's astrological signs laid out in a wide variety of materials**

ABOVE **The indirect method creates a smooth and hard-wearing surface that can withstand heavy traffic and last for years**

ABOVE **Pisces, the sign of the fish, is picked out in a mixture of pebbles and glazed tile against a background of small pieces**

111

SECTION 4

CHAPTER 9

A–Z plant directory

This plant directory does not claim to be an exhaustive list but it does include a good selection of plants that will give you the look and feel of a Mediterranean garden, wherever you live. The plants are listed alphabetically within the section that relates to their type (climber, flower, exotic or evergreen, etc.).

NAMING OF PLANTS

If the description is all in italics, this is a naturally occuring plant that has been discovered growing in habitat. For example, in *Allium aflatunense*, Allium is the genus name and aflatunense is the species name; this is a plant that was originally discovered growing in Central Asia, and therefore is a 'true' species. (Botanists find slight variations, so if you see f. or var. or subsp. these describe naturally occuring forms, varieties and subspecies.)

However, if you see a description like *Allium* 'White Giant', it tells you that the plant is a cultivar, and plant breeders and hybridizers have been selecting and crossing plants to produce and reproduce a distinctive plant that they can then name. Therefore, if you see a description that has 'xxx' after any name in this plant directory, you know that this is a cultivar and not a true species, so a place of origin will not be given.

Syn. is an abbreviation for 'synonym', which refers to the fact that the plant is well known by the alternative name.

HARDINESS RATINGS

The information given here, based on UK Royal Horticultural Society data, is on the cautious side, so if you are not prepared to take any chances, follow the hardiness ratings to the letter. Otherwise there is a great deal of leeway. Raised beds, good drainage, south-/south-west-facing borders and planting against a house wall all give plants a better habitat – so be prepared to experiment.

If you cannot bear to risk losing your most valued plants, keep back-ups by taking cuttings, lifting some of the plants and storing tubers, rhizomes, etc. under winter protection.

*	Half-hardy – down to 32°F/0°C
**	Frost-hardy – down to 23°F/–5°C
***	Fully hardy – down to 5°F/–15°C
(FT)	Frost-tender

SAFETY WARNING

Many plants can be harmful, both if eaten and as skin irritants, or because they are allergens and will aggravate asthma, eczema and other autoimmune disorders. Unless you are *absolutely certain* that they have a culinary use, do not eat them and be wary of skin contact, especially in bright sunlight. Tell your children that they should never eat anything out of the garden unless *you* have given it to them!

BULBS, CORMS, RHIZOMES, TUBERS

ABOVE **Agapanthus, or the African lily, has large and showy flowers; it is ideal for the border or for containers**

NAME: AGAPANTHUS (AFRICAN LILY)

Origin: S Africa
Type: Fully hardy to frost-hardy perennial
USDA zone: Typically Z7–9
Description: Strap-shaped leaves and large inflorescences of white or blue flowers; seed heads are decorative afterwards. Good for containers and in borders
Height and spread: 16in–5ft (41cm–1.5m) x 16–24in (41–61cm)
Popular species and varieties:
*A. campanulatus*** Grey-green leaves and rounded umbels of pale to dark blue, occasionally white, flowers. Height 24–48in (61–122cm), spread 18in (46cm). Z7
*A. 'Blue Giant'*** Umbels of deep-blue flowers. Height 4ft (1.2m), spread 24in (61cm). Z8
Where and how to grow: Rich, moist but well-drained soil in full sun. In containers use John Innes Number 3

Maintenance: Water well in the growing season and more sparingly in winter. Feed from spring until they have flowered
Propagation: Divide in spring
Tip: Choose the hybrids and cultivars rather than the species, as they are much hardier

NAME: ALLIUM (ORNAMENTAL ONION)

Origin: N hemisphere from dry and mountainous areas
Type: Fully hardy to frost-hardy perennials
USDA zone: Typically Z3–7
Description: These plants have stunning spherical flower heads in blue, white, and pink. They are very easy to grow and make a good early show in the border
Height and spread: 4in–6ft (10cm–1.8m) x 1–7in (2.5–18cm)
Popular species and varieties:
*A. aflatunense*** This has ribbed stems and linear mid-green leaves that measure approximately 12–24in (30–60cm) long. In the summer, 4in (10cm) long drumstick-like umbels of purple-pink flowers are produced. It has a clumping habit. Height 3ft (91cm), spread 4in (10cm). Z3
A. caeruleum, syn. *A. azureum*** The leaves die back before flowering. It produces dense

ABOVE **Alliums, the ornamental onions, are grown for their showy round flower heads, carried like colourful drumsticks**

umbels of bright blue-flowers on stiff stems during early summer. Height 24in (61cm), spread 1in (2.5cm). Z7/8

A. cristophii, syn. *A. albopilosum*** This has grey-green basal leaves which die back before flowering and 8in (20cm) wide umbels of interestingly bronze purple-pink flowers on stiff stems in early summer; dead heads are also showy. Height 12–24in (30–61cm), spread 6–7in (15–18cm). Z7/8

Where and how to grow: Plant bulbs in autumn (fall) at a depth of 2–4in (5–10cm). They like rich, moist but well-drained soil in full sun

Maintenance: Taller alliums may need support. They will gradually form clumps that should not

ABOVE **Cannas are one of the showiest flowers for a hot border, and their swordlike foliage is also striking and dramatic**

be disturbed unless you want to propagate the plant, or if the flowers become sparse

Propagation: Remove offset bulbs in autumn (fall)

NAME: CANNA (INDIAN SHOT PLANT)

Origin: Asia, tropical N and S America

Type: Half-hardy to frost-tender perennial

USDA zone: Typically Z8–9

Description: Fabulously showy plants, they are the quintessence of hot colour and extravagant display. They have been bred intensively for their flowers, so there is a huge choice of colour and height. They have large, paddle-shaped leaves that are 12–24in (30–61cm) long in bright green or dramatic maroon, referred to as 'brown leaf'

Height and spread: Dwarf varieties reach 16–24in (41–61cm) in height and giants reach 3–7ft (91cm–2.1m), both by a spread of 20in (51cm)

Popular species and varieties:

C. 'Black Knight'* This is a 'brown leaf' canna, which has bronze leaves and very dark-red flowers. Height reaches 6ft (1.8m), spread 20in (51cm). Z8/9

C. 'Picasso'* A green-leaf canna that has yellow flowers blotched with red. Height to 4ft (1.2m), spread 20in (51cm). Z8/9

C. indica 'Purpurea'* This is grown for its dark foliage as well as its orange-red flowers, as the deep-purple leaves make an excellent show in a border. Height 5–7ft (1.5–2.1m), spread 20in (51cm). Z8

Where and how to grow: They enjoy a fertile soil and sheltered site. In containers they like John Innes Number 3

Maintenance: Water well in the growing season and more sparingly in winter. They enjoy water in a dry spell. If you live in a frost-prone area the rhizomes should be lifted in the autumn (fall) and stored in barely moist peat or sand in a frost-free place. However, if you do want to experiment, we have never lifted our rhizomes, allowing the herbaceous growth to

ABOVE **There are attractive zantedeschia cultivars with colourful flowers, such as** *Zantedeschia aethiopica* **'Captain Samos'**

die down and protect the rhizomes instead; this has been very successful and we have large and ever-increasing clumps

Propagation: Divide the rhizomes in spring and grow in temperatures of 61°F/16°C. Water sparingly until they are growing well

Tip: They make a bold focus in the border or a very interesting container plant, though they won't grow to their full height in a pot

NAME: *ZANTEDESCHIA AETHIOPICA* (ARUM LILY)

Origin: S Africa

Type: Frost-hardy perennial

USDA zone: Typically Z8–9

Description: This beautiful plant has a clumping habit and is evergreen in mild areas. It has sword-shaped, bright-green leaves that grow to approximately 16in (41cm) long, and produces pure white flowers that are dramatic spathes, reaching 10in (25cm) long, with cream-coloured spikes within them

Height and spread: Both 16in (41cm)

Popular species and varieties:

There are some colourful new cultivars, but they are less vigorous and a little less hardy

Z. 'Captain Samos' ** Striking deep-yellow flowers with orange throats. Z8

Z. 'Gem' ** Translucent rose-pink flowers. Z7

Z. 'Schwarzwalder' ** Produces attractive dark-burgundy petals. Z8

Where and how to grow: They like a rich, moist soil in full sun. They can be grown as pond marginals in water up to 12in (30cm) deep. Grow from rhizomes

Maintenance: If the plants of *Zantedeschia aethiopica* are mulched well they will overwinter in most areas. Lift the cultivars and store them over the winter

Propagation: Divide in spring

CLIMBERS

NAME: *CAMPSIS RADICANS SYN. BIGNONIA RADICANS, TECOMA RADICANS* (TRUMPET VINE)

Origin: SE USA
Type: Frost-hardy perennial
USDA zone: Z7
Description: Vigorous climber and really exotic-looking but tough. It has much-divided leaves and terminal cymes of red blooms that are carried from midsummer to early autumn (fall)
Height and spread: 12ft (3.6m) x 6ft (1.8m) plus
Popular species and varieties:
C. radicans 'Yellow Trumpet' (also known as *C. radicans* f. *flava*) The same characteristics as *C. radicans* but produces yellow flowers
C. radicans 'Flamenco' This is as vigorous as its parent but has large pale-orange flowers
Where and how to grow: Fertile soil that is moist but well-drained in full sun against a wall. Grow from seed in a cold frame in autumn (fall)
Maintenance: Keep tying in the shoots as it grows. It will take up to three years for the

ABOVE **The trumpet vine, *Campsis radicans*, gives an exotic Mediterranean feel to the garden yet it is very easy to grow**

ABOVE *Ipomoea tricolor* 'Heavenly Blue', illustrated, will grow vigorously and flower profusely in one season from seed

framework to establish itself but from then onwards prune in late winter/early spring
Propagation: Root leaf-bud cuttings in spring or take semi-ripe cuttings in the summer

NAME: IPOMOEA (MORNING GLORY)

Origin: S America
Type: Half-hardy annuals or perennials grown as annuals
USDA zone: Z9–11
Description: This vigorous climber is lovely for pergolas, obelisks and walls, and great for late-summer flowers. There is plenty of colour choice from interesting cultivars
Height and spread: 6–15ft (1.8–4.6m) x 12in (30cm)
Popular species and varieties:
I. nil 'Scarlett O'Hara' Scarlet flowers with white throats. Height 15ft (4.5m), spread 12in (30cm)
I. purpurea 'Milky Way' White flowers with blue stripes. Height 6–10ft (1.8–3m), spread 12in (30cm)
I. purpurea 'Kniola's Purple-black' Purple-black flowers with red centres. Height 6–10ft (1.8–3m), spread 12in (30cm)
I. tricolor syn. *I. rubrocaerulea* Sky-blue flowers with white tubes, yellow at the base. Height 10–12ft (3–4m), spread 12in (30cm)

Where and how to grow: Grow from seed
Maintenance: Support the stems as they grow
Propagation: Grow from seed each year; it is worth collecting seed as it germinates well. After a mild winter, self-set seed will germinate

NAME: *TROPAEOLUM SPECIOSUM* (FLAME CREEPER, FLAME NASTURTIUM)

Origin: Chile
Type: Frost-hardy perennial
USDA zone: Z8–10
Description: This is a really special and individual species. It is a very attractive creeper which has dark-green hand-shaped leaves and carries scarlet flowers with long spurs from summer through to autumn (fall)
Height and spread: 10ft (3m) upwards x approx. 6ft (1.8m)
Where and how to grow: Likes a moist, rich soil that is neutral to acid in full sun with roots in shade. Ideally, grow on a south-facing wall
Maintenance: Support the stems as it climbs
Propagation: Can be divided in early spring

ABOVE *Tropaeolum speciosum* is a vigorous climber with brilliant red flowers and looks good grown through a dark hedge

ABOVE *Vitis vinifera* cultivars will grow and fruit in temperate zones, while ornamental vines are grown for foliage effects

NAME: VITIS (GRAPE VINE)

Origin: Woodland and woodland margins in N temperate regions
Type: Hardy perennial
USDA zone: Typically Z5–9
Description: Vineyards – with vines trained across wires on terraces over sun-baked hillsides – are iconic of Mediterranean gardens. Growing and fruiting them in temperate areas can be an interesting challenge. However, there are many easy-to-grow, hardy ornamental vines (with unpalatable fruits) that certainly give the sun-soaked look to your garden. Some have purple foliage all season; others flame with colour in autumn (fall)

119

Height and spread: 22–50ft (7–15m) x 6ft
(1.8m) plus

Popular species and varieties:

V. coignetiae Vigorous but very decorative
deciduous climber with inedible fruit. It has
large heart-shaped leaves, 12in (30cm) wide,
that become a rich red in autumn (fall). Height
50ft (15m), spread 6ft (1.8m) plus. Z7

V. vinifera 'Purpurea' For intense colour contrast
on your pergola, trellis or walls, etc., this
deciduous climber has 6in (15cm) long showy
purple leaves, turning an even deeper purple in
summer through to autumn (fall) when it
produces inedible fruit. Height 22ft (7m),
spread 6ft (1.8m) plus. Z7

Where and how to grow: Edible or inedible,
they like well-drained neutral to alkaline soil in
sun or partial shade. Grow from seed in
autumn (fall) or spring in a cold frame

Maintenance: Prune in midwinter and then
again in summer if necessary

Propagation: Take hardwood cuttings at the
end of winter or in early spring

ABOVE **Arctotis has striking, daisy-like flowers, freely produced all
summer, and it is also very easy to grow from seed**

FLOWERS

NAME: ARCTOTIS (VENIDIUM) (THE MONARCH OF THE VELDT)

Origin: S Africa

Type: Frost-tender perennial, grown as a half-
hardy annual

USDA zone: Z9–11

Description: It has hairy, silver leaves with
deep lobes that are 5in (13cm) long and
orange and white 4in (10cm) wide flowers
with deep-purple or black centres; they look a
bit like miniature sunflowers. There are lots of
interesting hybrids and cultivars that are
excellent for summer bedding and have been
bred to stay open for longer periods than the
species that close in the late afternoon and in
overcast weather

Height and spread: 18–24in (46–61cm)
x 12–16in (30–41cm)

Popular species and varieties:

A. x hybrida x Venidioarctotis (also known as
A. 'Harlequin Hybrids') These hybrids have
been bred for summer bedding, as they have
lobed, felty, silvery leaves that are 5in (13cm)
long, and they flower all summer, bearing a
variety of dark-centred red, yellow, pink,
orange or white flowers that measure 3–3½in
(8–9cm) across. Height 18–20in (46–51cm),
spread 12in (30cm)

A. venusta, syn. *A stoechadifolia* The blue-eyed
African daisy has 5in (13cm) long leaves, dark
green above and silver underneath, and
cream-coloured flower heads, 3in (8cm) across
with blue centres, carried from midsummer to
early autumn. Height 24in (61cm), spread
16in (41cm)

Where and how to grow: All arctotis like a
well-drained, moist, light soil in full sun. Grow
them from seed under cover and bed out when
frost danger has passed

Maintenance: Avoid disturbing the plants once
they are bedded out and deadhead regularly

Propagation: Grow from seed each year

ABOVE Ceanothus, the Californian lilac, has striking blue flowers and many cultivars, such as C. 'Tilden Park', shown here

NAME: *CEANOTHUS* (CALIFORNIAN LILAC)

Origin: California
Type: Fully hardy to frost-hardy perennials
USDA zone: From Z7–9
Description: Very variable, as there are both deciduous and evergreen species and cultivars, with a profusion of beautiful blue, pink and white flowers. They come in a variety of heights and forms, some good for training to a sunny wall, and they have flowering periods that run from spring, through summer and into autumn (fall)
Height and spread: 3–20ft (91cm–6.1m) x 5–12ft (1.5–3.6m)
Popular species and varieties:
C. 'Blue Mound'** A mound-forming shrub with leathery dark-green toothed leaves and mid-blue flowers that measure ¾in (2cm) across and are borne in profusion in late spring. Height 5ft (1.5m), spread 6ft (1.8m). Z8/9
C. 'Concha'** Good for training on a wall, this is a dense evergreen shrub with dark-green toothed leaves. The buds are reddish purple and open into masses of deep-blue flowers that measure 1¼in (3cm) across. 10ft (3m) height and spread. Z8/9
Where and how to grow: They can be grown from seed but this requires a lot of patience, so I would advise that you buy them in as established plants. They like a fertile soil and a sheltered site in full sun. They are lime-tolerant to a degree
Maintenance: Prune evergreens lightly after flowering and deciduous shrubs back to the desired basic shape and framework in early spring; if wall-grown, you should prune them after flowering or in late winter/early spring
Propagation: Take greenwood cuttings of deciduous and hardwood cuttings of evergreens in spring/summer
Tip: If grown against a sheltered wall they will achieve twice the height

ABOVE Cistus, like *Cistus x purpureus,* here, with profuse and lovely, though short-lived, flowers, are a must for the Mediterranean garden

NAME: CISTUS (ROCK ROSE OR SUN ROSE)

Origin: Canary Islands, N Africa, Turkey and S Europe
Type: Frost-hardy perennial shrub
USDA zone: Z8–9
Description: Confusingly sharing the common name of rock or sun rose with helianthemum, these evergreen shrubs grow in dry and stony soils. They can be short-lived but are treasured for their ephemeral papery flowers, which each last only one day but are produced in profusion
Height and spread: 3–6ft (91cm–1.8m) x 3–5ft (91cm–1.5m), with some miniatures at only 30in (76cm) x 36in (91cm)
Popular species and varieties:
Cistus x purpureus (*C. creticus* x *C. ladanifer*) Lance-shaped or oval leaves with wavy edges. Crinkled deep-pink flowers in the summer that are up to 3in (8cm) wide. 3ft (91cm) height and spread. Z8–9

C x argenteus 'Silver Pink' Moundlike shrub with dark-green leaves and silvery-pink flowers, 3in (8cm) wide, with yellow centres. Height 30in (76cm), spread 36in (91cm). Z8
Where and how to grow: You can raise them from seed in spring and they will grow quite quickly, flowering well in their second year. They prefer a poor to fairly fertile, well-drained soil in full sun. They will tolerate a limey soil
Maintenance: Prune lightly, as they do not like hard pruning. However, they do become leggy in time, so it is best to treat them as short-lived plants and take cuttings
Propagation: Propagate from seed or softwood cuttings. Take greenwood cuttings in the summer

NAME: DELOSPERMA SPECIES

Origin: S Africa
Type: Half-hardy to frost-hardy perennial
USDA zone: Z7–8
Description: The mat-forming succulent

ABOVE *Delosperma cooperi* flowers in carpets and curtains of brilliant lilac from May right through to the first frosts

delosperma has leaves in triangular or cylindrical sections and daisy-like flowers in shades from pale pink to magenta, sometimes with bright-yellow centres

Height and spread: 2–5in (5–13cm) x 24in (61cm) to indefinite

Popular species and varieties:

D. cooperi** This is a great plant that will create spreading carpets and produce curtains of colour on pond edges and over the edges of raised beds; it is also good in containers. The leaves are fat and light green, and it has bright magenta flowers, measuring 2in (5cm) across, which begin in late spring and continue in sheets of colour until the first frosts. It is reputed to be hardy to17°F/ −8°C, but we have had prolonged cold weather down to 14°F/−10°C and the plant has been fine. Z7–8

Height 2in (5cm), spread 24in (61cm) plus

D. lydenburgense** This succulent has fleshy, bright-green leaves. It is evergreen apart from

the coldest winters. Also good for clothing pond edges, rockery sites, raised beds and for carpeting. It produces 2½in (6cm) beautiful, bright-yellow, daisy-like flowers for two or three weeks in late spring and then intermittently for the rest of the spring and summer. Height 2in (5cm), spread 24in (61cm) plus. Z8

Where and how to grow: They prefer a gravelly, well-drained soil and a sheltered site in full sun. Grow from seed at 70°F/21°C

Maintenance: Keep an eye on the clumps and divide them if they begin to overrun their position

Propagation: Take stem cuttings in spring and summer. Keep them in a dry place for 10–14 days before planting them up, to ensure that they do not rot. Plants can be divided

Tip: Take cuttings and overwinter them in a frost-free place in colder areas

NAME: *DOROTHEANTHUS BELLIDIFORMIS* (SYN. *MESEMBRYANTHEMUM CRINIFLORUM*) (LIVINGSTONE DAISY OR ICE PLANT)

Origin: S Africa
Type: Half-hardy annual
USDA zone: Z11
Description: You can get a very similar look to the carpeting delosperma, described above, by growing the annual mixed Livingstone Daisy, with its fleshy leaves and riot of daisy-like flowers in red, yellow, white, and pink, carried throughout summer

Height and spread: 3–6in (8–15cm) x 12in (30cm)

Popular species and varieties:
There is a range of seed mixes readily available each year:

D. bellidiformis 'Magic Carpet' Produces flowers in pink, purple, orange and white. Height 3in (8cm), spread 12in (30cm)

D. bellidiformis 'Gelato White' Pure white flowers. Height 4in (10cm), spread 12in (30cm)

D. bellidiformis 'Gelato Dark Pink' Produces deep-pink flowers. Height 4in (10cm), spread 12in (30cm)

123

ABOVE *Dorotheanthus bellidiformis*, the annual Livingstone daisy, is perfect for giving you quick colour with a really exotic feel

Where and how to grow: Grow from seed under glass and bed out when the danger of frost has passed. They like a poor, gritty soil in full sun

Maintenance: Deadhead regularly

Propagation: Grow from seed each year

NAME: *ERIGERON KARVINSKIANUS* SYN. *E. MUCRONATUS* (MEXICAN DAISY)

Origin: Mexico to Panama

Type: Hardy perennial

USDA zone: Z7

Description: This pretty, spreading plant, with a proliferation of daisy-like flowers, is widely naturalized in Mediterranean-climate areas and in the south-west of England. The flowers start off as white with yellow centres then fade through to pink

Height and spread: 6–12in (15–30cm) x 20in–3ft (51–91cm) or more

Popular species and varieties:
E. karvinskianus 'Profusion' A particularly profuse-flowering cultivar, with pink or white flower heads. Height 8–12in (20–30cm), spread 20in (50cm)

Where and how to grow: They like a well-drained fertile soil in full sun. Grow from seed in a cold frame in spring

Maintenance: To encourage more flowers, deadhead them regularly. Cut the plant down in autumn (fall) to avoid straggly growth and divide the clumps every couple of years

Propagation: Divide the plants and/or grow from basal cuttings in spring

Tip: This is an excellent plant for paving stones, walls and stair risers

NAME: ESCHSCHOLZIA SPECIES (CALIFORNIAN POPPY)

Origin: California
Type: Hardy annual
USDA zone: Z7
Description: A real splash of sunshine in the garden, they produce a profusion of short-lived but abundant glossy orange and yellow flowers above divided ferny foliage. There are lots of attractive cultivars available in double and frilled varieties and in an appetizing range of delicate colours
Height and spread: 6–12in (15–30cm) x 6in (15cm)
Popular species and varieties:
E. caespitosa Delicate and smaller with fine, threadlike foliage and many single bright-yellow flowers that measure 1¼–2in (3–5cm) across. 6in (15cm) height and spread
E. californica Finely divided blue-green to grey leaves and numerous single flowers that measure up to 3in (8cm) across. Usually orange, the flowers can be also be yellow,

ABOVE Annual *Eschscholzia californica* provides waves of rich colour, and looks particularly good among spiky exotics

cream and white. Height 1ft (30cm), spread 6in (15cm)
There are lots of interesting mixes like:
E. californica 'Thai Silk Mixed' This pretty mix has silky and wavy-edged petals in shades of red, pink and orange. Height 10in (25cm), spread 6in (15cm)

ABOVE Daisy-flowered *Erigeron karvinskianus* is a vigorous, trouble-free little perennial and excellent for softening paving and stairs

125

E. californica 'Stawberry Fields' Fluted petals in shades of red and yellow. Height 10in (25cm), spread 6in (15cm)

Where and how to grow: They like a poor, well-drained soil in full sun. Grow from seed in mid-spring to early autumn (fall)

Maintenance: Deadhead regularly to prolong the flowering period

Propagation: They self-seed readily, so after the first year you will have flowers from spring to autumn (fall)

NAME: FELICIA SPECIES

Origin: S Africa

Type: Annuals and tender perennials grown as annuals

USDA zone: Z8–9

Description: Rounded and bushy with deep-green leaves and dark or pale-blue flower heads, 1–2in (2.5–5cm) across, borne throughout summer and into autumn (fall)

Height and spread: Both 12–24in (30–61cm)

Popular species and varieties:

F. amelloides (Blue Daisy) Rounded and bushy with blue flower heads carried from summer through to autumn (fall). There is a particularly attractive form that has variegated leaves. 12–24in (30–60cm) height and spread. Z9

F. bergeriana (Kingfisher Daisy) This has a mat-forming habit, lance-shaped leaves, and bright-blue flower heads that measure approximately 1¼in (3cm) across, with yellow centres. 10in (25cm) height and spread. Z8

Where and how to grow: They prefer a poor to fairly fertile, well-drained soil and a position that is in full sun. Grow from seed under protection during the spring

Maintenance: To keep a compact plant you will need to deadhead them regularly and pinch out young shoots

Propagation: Grow each year from seed

Tip: They don't like to stay damp

ABOVE **The foliage of this variegated *Felicia amelloides*, a South African blue daisy, is particularly attractive**

NAME: GAZANIA CULTIVARS

Origin: Africa

Type: Half-hardy to frost-tender (they can withstand a small amount of frost) perennials, usually grown as annuals

USDA zone: Z9

Description: They have lance-shaped, often feltlike, leaves and large, daisy-like flowers in a range of bright colours with dark centres. They flower throughout summer

Height and spread: Both to 10in (25cm)

Popular species and varieties:

They have been widely hybridized, so look for: Gazania Chansonette Series* and Gazania Daybreak Series* – These have dark-green leaves with silvery undersides. Flowers are zoned in contrasting colours in shades of pink, orange, yellow and bronze. Height 8in (20cm), spread 10in (25cm)

Gazania Talent Series* – These have 6in (15cm) long, attractive, feltlike grey leaves and yellow, orange or pink flowers. Height 8in (20cm), spread 10in (25cm)

There are also named single colours, such as G. 'Daybreak Bronze'* and G. 'Talent Yellow'*, plus some cuttings-derived cultivars including flashy G. 'Aztec'* with yellow centres and cream and red petals, and double-flowered G. 'Yellow Buttons'*. All have a 10in (25cm) height and spread

Where and how to grow: Poor, well-drained soil in full sun. Grow from seed in spring with protection and bed out after the frosts are past

Maintenance: Prolong the flowering season by deadheading

Propagation: Grow from seed. Ours self-seed freely and appear the following year

NAME: HELIANTHEMUM (ROCK ROSE OR SUN ROSE)

Origin: Largely a Mediterranean genus

Type: Hardy perennial

USDA zone: Z7

ABOVE Gazanias are desirable South African daisies with a great choice of colours, like *Gazania* Daybreak 'Red Stripe', shown here

ABOVE Helianthemums, like this *H.* 'Henfield Brilliant', are another of the staples for the Mediterranean flower garden

127

Description: This is a shrubby evergreen or semi-evergreen plant that is grown for its colourful saucer-shaped flowers, carried in profusion over a long period. There are many worthwhile cultivars and hybrids

Height and spread: 8–12in (20–30cm) x 8–18in (20–46cm)

Popular species and varieties:

H. 'Ben Nevis' Dark-green leaves and orange-yellow flowers with deeper centres. 8in (20cm) height and spread

H. 'Henfield Brilliant' Salmon-red flowers, grey-green leaves. Height 8–12in (20–30cm), spread 12in (30cm)

H. 'Wisley Primrose' Grey-green leaves and pale-yellow flowers. Height to 12in (30cm), spread 18in (46cm)

Where and how to grow: They enjoy a moderately fertile neutral or alkaline soil in a sunny, well-drained position. Species can be raised from seed in a cold frame in the spring

ABOVE **South African red-hot pokers, like this Kniphofia cultivar, are very easy to grow and provide dazzling colour**

Maintenance: After shoots have flowered, cut back to within 1in (2.5cm) of the old growth

Propagation: Take softwood cuttings in spring and summer

NAME: KNIPHOFIA (RED HOT POKER)

Origin: S Africa

Type: Hardy perennial

USDA zone: Typically Z5–7

Description: Spiky green leaves and dramatic flowers in orange, red, cream, yellow and green. They are easy to grow and look excellent in a hot-coloured garden

Height and spread: 16in–6ft (41cm–1.8m) x 18in–3ft (46–91cm)

Popular species and varieties:

Try a simple mix with Kniphofia mixed hybrids or named cultivars in various heights and colours, such as:

K. 'Green Jade' This is a robust evergreen with green flowers in late summer/early autumn (fall), which progress from cream to white. Height 5ft (1.5m), spread 24–30in (61–76cm). Z5

K. 'Little Maid' This is a tiny deciduous plant with narrow, grasslike leaves, and green buds opening to cream then white in late summer to early autumn (fall). Height 24in (61cm), spread 18in (46cm). Z6

K. 'Prince Igor' Deciduous, with deep-orange spires of flowers in early to mid-autumn (fall). Height 6ft (1.8m), spread 36in (91cm). Z7

K. 'Sunningdale Yellow' Deciduous, with long-lasting spires of slender, primrose-yellow flowers, produced in summer. Height 36in (91cm), spread 18in (46cm). Z7

Where and how to grow: A rich and moist but well-drained soil in full sun or partial shade

Maintenance: Mulch the plants during their first winter

Propagation: You can collect seed, but it is unlikely to be true to the parent. Divide large clumps in late spring or take basal cuttings from new shoots

ABOVE Lampranthus are great for dazzling colour, but they will need overwintering under glass in frost-prone areas

NAME: LAMPRANTHUS

Origin: S Africa
Type: Tender perennial
USDA zone: Z8–10
Description: These mat-forming succulents have originated in semi-desert areas. They have narrow, succulent leaves and are grown for their colourful, daisy-like flowers, which are borne in profusion throughout summer
Height and spread: 12–20in (30–51cm) x indefinite spread
Popular species and varieties:
L. aurantiacus This has orange flowers and grey-green leaves. Height 18in (46cm), indefinite spread. Z9–10
L. roseus syn. *Mesembryanthemum multiradiatum** Very pretty purple flowers are carried throughout summer on this low-growing

mesembryanthemum, which has clumping grey-green leaves. Height can reach 20in (51cm), indefinite spread. Z9–11
There are also lots of cultivars in various colours, like apricot, pink, red and yellow.
Where and how to grow: These plants like poor soil in a sunny, well-drained site. They are able to survive in mild areas (treat as half-hardy elsewhere) and *L. spectabilis* has naturalized in the south-west of England. Grow from seed in temperatures of at least 66–75°F/19–24°C
Maintenance: Lift and overwinter them in frost-free conditions or take cuttings to overwinter under glass
Propagation: Take cuttings, as for delosperma (see pages 122–3), during late spring and summer

ABOVE **There are lots of cultivars to choose, like** *Lavatera arborea* **'Bredon Springs', all bred from the Mediterranean parent**

NAME: *LAVATERA ARBOREA* (TREE MALLOW)

Origin: Mediterranean
Type: Frost-hardy perennial
USDA zone: Z7–8
Description: Short-lived evergreen shrub with 8in (20cm) long leaves and profuse racemes of funnel-shaped pink or lavender flowers during the summer.
Height and spread: 6–10ft (1.8–3m) x 5–6ft (1.5–1.8m)
Popular species and varieties:
L. arborea 'Variegata' Grown for its brightly green and white variegated leaves.
There are lots of coloured cultivars, with white, pink and bicoloured flowers. Height 10ft (3m), spread 5ft (1.5m). Z8

L. 'Bredon Springs' This is a vigorous semi-evergreen plant, with grey-green leaves and pink flowers flushed mauve. 6ft (1.8m) height and spread. Z7–9
Where and how to grow: Enjoys a sunny and sheltered site in light, fairly fertile soil
Maintenance: Prune back to the permanent framework in early spring
Propagation: Take softwood cuttings in spring/summer

NAME: OSTEOSPERMUM CULTIVARS AND SPECIES

Origin: S Africa & the Arabian peninsula
Type: Half-hardy perennial, often grown as an annual
USDA zone: Z7–9
Description: Another iconic African daisy-like flower. The flower head is known as composite, with a contrasting centre of tiny disc florets (individual flowers) ringed by ray florets, which can be spoon-shaped and have contrasting undersides. There are plenty of mixed hybrids available in seeds, plants and selected cultivars
Height and spread: 4–24in (10–61cm) x 24–36in (61–91cm)
Popular species and varieties:
O. 'Buttermilk' This has 2in (5cm) wide flower heads with pale-yellow ray florets, which are white at the base, deep yellow underneath, and have deep-blue centres. 24in (61cm) height and spread. Z9
O. jucundum Has 2in (5cm) wide flower heads with purple-pink ray florets, deeper underneath, and deep purple centres. Height 4–20in (10–51cm), spread 20–36in (51–91cm). Z7–9
O. 'Whirlygig' Has 2–3in (5–8cm) wide flower heads with attractive spoon-shaped white ray florets, deep-blue underneath, with deep-blue centres. 24in (61cm) height and spread. Z8
Where and how to grow: They like light but fertile soil in a sunny and sheltered position
Maintenance: Deadhead to prolong flowering. In frost-prone areas overwinter under glass

ABOVE **Like gazanias, osteospermums are easy-to-grow African daisies, with lots of options like this *Osteospermum* 'Buttermilk'**

Propagation: From seed in spring under glass until frost danger has passed. Take softwood cuttings in late spring, semi-ripe cuttings during late summer

NAME: PELARGONIUM

Origin: S Africa
Type: Half-hardy perennial
USDA zone: Z9–10
Description: These are the best container plants, as they are cheap and cheerful, relatively drought-resistant, and they bring an instant splash of warm Mediterranean colour to your garden in pots, window boxes and hanging baskets. The choices available could furnish a reference book on their own: about 20 species have acted as the parents to hundreds of cultivars, which are then divided and subdivided into several groups; so you should choose the colours and shapes that most suit your requirements.

ABOVE **Pelargoniums are probably the best choice for an abundant, colourful and low-maintenance display in summer containers**

Popular species and varieties:
Zonal pelargoniums are perhaps the ones most of us think of. They are upright plants with rounded leaves 1½–5½in (4–14cm) across, which have bands or zones of bronze and maroon. They flower profusely all summer. The flowers measure 1in (2.5cm) across and come in shades of red, purple, pink and white. There are many different flower shapes and also fancy-leaved foliage types. Zonal pelargoniums are either grown from seed as F1 hybrids, which come true from seed and grow and flower in a year, or as large-flowered cultivars, raised only from cuttings. Height up to 24in (61cm), spread up to 12in (30cm)
Other useful groups include the ivy-leaved group, which comprises trailing evergreens that are therefore ideal for hanging baskets and window boxes or for planting to trail over the edges of containers. They have clusters of single to double flowers that are up to 1½in (4cm) in diameter and available in red, pink, lilac, purple or white. Again, they flower all summer long. Height to 10–12in (25–30cm), and they can reach up to 3ft (1m) spread
The scented-leaves group consists of numerous cultivars with their own distinctive fragrances when the leaves are brushed, so these plants are a good choice for edging steps and doorways where they will be brushed against. They have mid-green and variegated aromatic leaves, and bear profuse clusters of single flowers measuring 1in (2.5cm) across in lilac, pink, purple and white all summer long. Height 18–20in (46–51cm), spread 10–12in (25–30cm)

Where and how to grow: They like a sunny position, though the zonal pelargonium will tolerate a certain amount of shade. The F1 seeds give fine plants in one growing season; they come true from seed and produce mainly single flowers. Sow F1 seed at 55–64°C/13–18°C in late winter/early spring. Bedded out they like a well-drained fertile soil that is neutral to alkaline

Maintenance: Pelargoniums are relatively drought-tolerant container plants and need to be watered moderately when in growth and sparingly in the winter. Deadhead regularly. Overwinter in a dry and frost-free place

Propagation: The large-flowered cultivars can only be propagated from cuttings, which can be overwintered as house or conservatory plants and used outside in the summer. Take softwood cuttings in spring, summer and early autumn (fall)

ABOVE The Mediterranean phlomis are very showy, though *Phlomis purpurea* is not as hardy as its yellow cousin, *P. fruticosa*

NAME: PHLOMIS SPECIES

Origin: Europe, N Africa and Asia
Type: Fully hardy to frost-hardy perennial
USDA zone: Z7–8
Description: These are sagelike plants, originating in dry and rocky areas. They have

grey-green to light-green, often hairy, leaves and hooded dead-nettle-like flowers

Height and spread: 24in–3ft (61–91cm) x 24in–5ft (61cm–1.5m)

Popular species and varieties:

P. fruticosa∗∗∗ borderline (Jersualem Sage) An evergreen shrub, creating mounds of wrinkly greyish-green leaves. In early summer to midsummer it bears golden, hooded, tubular flowers in whorls around upright stems. Height 3ft (91cm), spread 5ft (1.5m). Z7

P. purpurea∗∗ The greyish-green leaves are leathery, with hairy surfaces and woolly undersides; the shoots are also woolly. It has purple to pink flowers, occasionally white, which are 1in (2.5cm) long. 24in (61cm) height and spread. Z8

Where and how to grow: Likes a position in full sun. Sow seed in spring in a fertile soil with good drainage

Maintenance: Lightly trim the plants after flowering to keep a good shape

Propagation: Divide in spring or autumn (fall). Take softwood cuttings in summer

Note: It is a high irritant

NAME: SALVIA SPECIES (SAGE)

Origin: They have a wide geographical spread but favour sunny sites

Type: Half-hardy and hardy perennials, plus biennials

USDA zone: Z5–11

Description: They are usually aromatic and often hairy, much-loved by bees, with two-lipped flowers in a range of colours, including pinks and blues. They can provide a subtle cloud of flowers in the border

Height and spread: 18in–5ft (46cm–1.5m) x 12in–3ft (30cm–91cm)

Popular species and varieties:

S. guaranitica 'Purple Majesty'∗ Wrinkly, mid-green leaves, branching stems, and purple flowers carried in late summer to autumn (fall). Height 5ft (1.5m), spread 24in (61cm). Z8

ABOVE **Although it is really dramatic, *Salvia sclarea* is easy to grow with aromatic foliage and tall spires of flowers**

S. involucrata ∗∗ Soft hairs on rich-green leaves, purplish-red flowers with pink bracts, carried in late summer to autumn (fall). Height 5ft (1.5m), spread 3ft (91cm). Z8–9

S. sclarea∗∗∗ Aromatic, with hairy, oval, wrinkled, mid-green leaves that are up to 9in (23cm) long. In late spring through to the summer it produces tall panicles or racemes of pastel flowers in lilac, pink or blue, with lilac bracts. The flowers uncurl over a few days into tall spires which make a real statement. Height 3ft (91cm), spread 12in (30cm). Z5

Where and how to grow: Grow from seed in a sunny, well-drained position. Hairy species like a sharp drainage and full sun

Maintenance: Prune lightly to shape in spring

Propagation: Divide perennials in spring and take basal or softwood cuttings in spring/early summer. Take semi-ripe cuttings in summer and autumn (fall)

NAME: *SEDUM SPECTABILE* (ICE PLANT)

Origin: China, Korea
Type: Hardy perennial
USDA Zone: From Z4
Description: A deciduous plant with upright stems and toothed grey-green leaves, grown for its fabulous heads of flowers which measure up to 6in (15cm) across and are borne in late summer; they are irresistible to bees and butterflies. The heads will persist as skeletal architectural focal points until you cut them back
Height and spread: Both 18in (46cm)
Popular species and varieties:
Many lovely cultivars have been bred, including:
S. spectabile 'Album' This has attractive pure white flowers

ABOVE *Sedum spectabile* is a useful perennial for late-flowering colour, with many cultivars, like this pink 'Brilliant'

S. spectabile 'Brilliant' This is quite dramatic, as it has very bright-pink petals and darker-red centres
S. spectabile 'Bertram Anderson' A very showy plant with purple foliage and flowers
S. spectabile 'Purpureum' This cultivar has beautiful red flowers
S. spectabile 'Vera Jameson' Showy with purple foliage and pink flowers
S. spectabile 'Aureovariegata' Striking with its pink flowers and variegated foliage
Where and how to grow: Grow in a well-drained soil, neutral to slightly alkaline is preferred, in full sun
Maintenance: Cut back after flowering to keep a pleasing shape, and divide every couple of years to maintain vigour
Propagation: Divide in spring and take softwood cuttings in summer

(See also carpeting hardy sedums below)

NAME: CARPETING HARDY SEDUMS (STONECROP)

Origin: Widely distributed in mountainous areas of the N hemisphere and in S America
Type: Hardy perennial
USDA zone: From Z4
Description: These low-growing and mat-forming species have fleshy foliage in shades of grey, grass-green and purple, and bear masses of yellow, white or pink flowers during the summer. They are good in containers, for growing in gravel and paving, along the edges of raised beds and ponds, and for softening stair risers
Height and spread: 2in (5cm) x 24in (61cm) plus
Popular species and varieties:
There is an enormous choice, but some of the best include:
S. acre (Biting or Common Stonecrop) A bright splash of colour. This evergreen has dense, spreading shoots, clothed in tiny, fleshy, pale-

ABOVE *S. album* 'Coral Carpet' foreground, *S. spathulifolium* var. *purpureum* centre and *S. acre* right (with *Delosperma nubigenum* at back)

green leaves and carries an abundance of small yellow flowers. Z5

S. acre 'Aureum' This is a larger form with variegated green and golden leaves. Z5

S. album (White Stonecrop) Small leaves with blunt ends. Variable in colour depending on where it is grown: the leaves are lush and green in wetter conditions and red and bronze in drier positions. Vigorous and drought-resistant. Z4

S. album 'Coral Carpet' A brighter cultivar with small rounded or cylindrical leaves in red and maroon and small white flowers. Z6

Where and how to grow: Grow species from seed and cultivars from named plants. They like a fairly poor soil that is well drained and neutral to alkaline in full sun

Maintenance: Cut back clumps if they are becoming too large, and look out for invasive weeds growing among them

Propagation: Divide in spring, take cuttings in summer, as for delosperma (pages 122–3)

EXOTICS
NAME: OPUNTIA SPECIES

Origin: N, C and S America
Type: Half-hardy to frost-hardy perennials
USDA zone: Z8–10
Description: Cacti with padlike, flattened, oval, round or cylindrical branches and spines that grow from areoles on the surface. Older plants produce cup-shaped flowers which are usually yellow but occasionally red, followed by prickly, sometimes edible, fruits. Many make good subjects for dramatic outside planting schemes

Height and spread: There are some miniscule specimens, but those suitable for garden planting vary from 4in–15ft (10cm–5m) in height and 3–15ft (91cm–5m) spread

Popular species and varieties:
We have grown the following tall upright species as frost-hardy perennials – hardy to

135

ABOVE **You can get the look of this Spanish garden near Malaga by growing prickly pear (opuntia species) in your garden**

14F (−10°C) − but for details on how to grow them, see below

O. basilaris Clumping, with blue-grey stems made up of rounded segments, each 4–8in (10–20cm) long. The areoles bear fine spines, surrounded by brown glochids. It has purple-red flowers, 2in (5cm) wide, and green fruits. Height 3ft (91cm), spread 30in (76cm) plus. Z8

O. chlorotica Bushy cactus with blue-green pads, 8in (20cm) long, and grey areoles with yellow glochids and one to six yellow spines which darken with time. It has yellow flowers with red outsides, 3in (8cm) across, and purple fruits. Height 6ft (1.8m), spread 30in (76cm). Z8

O. engelmannii Bushy with flat grey-green or mid-green pads, which are 4–16in (10–41cm) long, and white areoles with yellow glochids and one or two spines. It produces attractive cup-shaped yellow flowers, followed by edible and spineless fruits. 15ft (4.6m) height and spread. Z8

Where and how to grow: A sheltered sunny spot, like a rockery against a south-facing wall. Wetness rather than cold damages cacti in cold months, so plant in a raised bed with very sharp drainage. Grow from seed during spring

Maintenance: Keep them well weeded, as once invasive weeds get a hold it is difficult to eradicate them. Cut back in the growing season if they are outgrowing their space

Propagation: Remove pads between late spring and early autumn (fall), keep them in a dry, warm place for two weeks while a callous forms, then pot them into gritty, slightly moist compost to grow on

Tip: In colder areas, plunge pots of cacti into outside beds in the summer months and keep them under glass in a frost-free place in the winter months. If you decide to experiment with leaving your cacti out, plant them out early in the season, once the danger of frost has passed, so that they are well established before the winter. Also keep a supply of cuttings under cover in case of losses

Note: Handle with care, as they almost all have irritating spines

NAME: AGAVE SPECIES (CENTURY PLANT)

Origin: N, C and S America

Type: Frost-tender to frost-hardy and half-hardy perennials

USDA zone: Z8–10

Description: Succulent rosette-forming plants with rigid fleshy leaves and toothed edges, often tipped with sharp spines. Excellent for containers and as focal-point architectural plants

Height and spread: Both 20in–6ft (51cm–1.8m)

Popular species and varieties:

*A. americana** Basal rosettes of thick, leathery blue-green leaves, 6ft (1.8m) long, with sharp terminal spines. Will survive in a sharply drained site. Height 6ft (1.8m), spread 10ft (3m). Z8 Its showy cultivars, which certainly need winter protection, include:

A. americana 'Variegata' (FT) This has yellow edges to the leaves. Z9

A. americana 'Mediopicta' (FT) Has a yellow inner stripe. Z9

A. americana 'Mediopicta Alba' (FT) Has a white inner stripe. Z9

ABOVE *Agave americana* 'Variegata' is an excellent and dramatic container plant but it needs winter protection from frost

*A. parryi** Compact with broad, spiny, greyish-blue leaves that are up to 12in (30cm) long. It will survive in a well-drained position. Height 20in (51cm), spread 3ft (91cm). Z7

Where and how to grow: A sheltered sunny spot, such as a rockery against a south-facing wall, would be ideal. Often it is wetness rather than cold that causes damage, so they need a raised bed with very sharp drainage, and to be planted at an angle so that water does not collect in the rosettes. Grow from seed during spring

Maintenance: Keep them well weeded, as once invasive weeds get a hold it is difficult and painful to eradicate them

Propagation: Remove rooted offsets between late spring and early autumn (fall), and pot them into gritty, slightly moist compost to grow on

Tip: In colder areas, plunge them into pots in outside beds in the summer months and keep them under glass in a frost-free place during the winter months. They are also excellent container plants for the summer patio. They can go inside as interesting and exotic houseplants or you can lift them, and store them in any dry,

frost-free place like a garage or shed. If you leave them outside, make sure you have a supply of rooted offsets as a back-up

NAME: CITRUS SPECIES

Origin: S E Asia and E Pacific
Type: Half-hardy, frost-hardy and frost-tender perennials, but they may stand short periods at 32°F (0°C)
USDA zone: Typically Z9–10
Description: These are evergreen trees and shrubs with glossy green foliage and shallow cup-shaped flowers which are often fragrant. They bear aromatic fruits. Blossom and fruit can be carried on the same plant at the same time. All of the citrus fruits make very attractive container plants for the summer months and bring a touch of the exotic to your garden.

ABOVE Citrus are ideal for a Mediterranean feel in containers overwintered inside, or as specimen plants in a warmer garden

137

They will flower and set fruit, but the fruit is unlikely to be large and palatable in a temperate area unless it is kept in a conservatory over winter

Height and spread: As container plants they will probably not achieve much more than 6ft (1.8m) in height and 3ft (91cm) spread, though in favourable frost-free areas planted in the ground they will reach 6–30ft (1.8–9.1m) in height and a spread of 5–20ft (1.5–6.1m)

Popular species and varieties:

C. aurantium (Seville Orange) (FT) A spiny oval tree with mid-green leaves, fragrant white flowers from late spring to summer that measure ¾in (2cm) across, and red-tinged orange fruits, approximately 2–3in (5–8cm) in size. Height 30ft (9.1m), spread 20ft (6.1m) in a favourable position in the ground. Z9

C. limon (Lemon) (FT) A big shrub or small tree with light-green leaves, scented flowers that measure 1½–2in (4–5cm) across, and oval yellow fruits that are 3–6in (8–15cm) large Height 6–22ft (1.8–7m), spread 5–10ft (1.5–3m). Z10

C. reticulata (Clementine, Mandarin, Tangerine) (FT) Spiny large shrub or small tree with deep-green leaves, highly scented flowers 1–1½in (2.5–4cm) across and rounded orange fruit that measure 1½–3in (4–8cm). Height 6–25ft (1.8–7.6m), spread 5–10ft (1.5–3m). Z9

Where and how to grow: Plant them in large containers in a rich loam-based compost like John Innes Number 3. Overwinter them under glass. Outside they like moist, well-drained, acid-to-neutral, moderately rich soil in full sun

Maintenance: In containers, water freely and give them a feed with liquid fertilizer every three weeks or so. Move to a frost-free place over winter, reduce watering and cut them back in winter or spring, if necessary. Outside in frost-free regions, prune when dormant to keep a good framework

Propagation: Root semi-ripe cuttings during the summer

NAME: *OLEA EUROPAEA* (OLIVE)

Origin: Mediterranean
Type: Frost-hardy perennial
USDA zone: Z9
Description: This is a unique slow-growing evergreen shrub or small tree with grey-green-surfaced leaves that have silvery undersides, bearing small, white, fragrant flowers and setting edible green fruit which ripens to black in warmer areas
Height and spread: Both 30ft (9.1m) max.
Where and how to grow: Grow in deep and fertile but very well-drained soil in full sun. They are a good container subject

ABOVE *Olea europaea*, the olive, is a great choice for a specimen tree in a warm, sheltered courtyard or in containers

Maintenance: Prune out branches to create a main stem, otherwise it will remain bushy and shrubby

Propagation: Take semi-ripe cuttings during the summer

NAME: PHORMIUM CULTIVARS (NEW ZEALAND FLAXES)

Origin: New Zealand
Type: Hardy perennial
USDA zone: Z8
Description: There are plenty of colourful cultivars among these evergreens, which are grown for their bold, sword-shaped leaves. They are architectural plants, ideal for patios, tubs and interesting garden arrangements. Large-growing varieties make huge architectural subjects, while the dwarf forms are perfect for containers. Taller forms can be used to make a dramatic screen or hedge. Their tall spikes of abundant orange flowers are carried on naked stems

Height and spread: Both 13in–6ft (33cm–1.8m)

Popular species and varieties:
P. 'Apricot Queen' An outstanding dwarf form, with cream leaves flushed apricot when young, maturing to a pale creamy yellow with green and bronze margins. 30in (76cm) height and spread

P. 'Platt's Black' A dramatic and extremely dark purple-black weeping variety. 3ft (91cm) height and spread

P. 'Sunset' A medium-sized and erect grower, with bronze leaves overlaid with pastel shades of gold and apricot-pink with green stripes and margins. 5ft (1.5m) height and spread

P. 'Rainbow Maiden' (also known as 'Maori Maiden') Very showy, with delicate weeping leaves in rich, rosy salmon-pink to coral-red, banded with bronze margins. 30in (76cm) height and spread

P. cookianum 'Tricolor' A magnificent plant, with broad, arching leaves striped vertically rich-green in the centre, creamy-yellow stripes

ABOVE **Tough phormium cultivars make a really good framework planting in gardens, as they have structure and evergreen colour**

towards the edge and bright-red margins. 4ft (1.2m) height and spread

P. 'Yellow Wave' This is a vigorous plant. It has green leaves with a drooping habit and develops strong pale-yellow variegation after the first few inches (5–7.5cm) of growth. Height and spread reaching 3ft (91cm)

Where and how to grow: Phormiums enjoy a well-drained and fairly fertile soil in sun, though they will tolerate poor soil in shade. They are slow from seed, so it is better to buy in a plant

Maintenance: Feed and water in the growing season for maximum growth. A protective mulch of gravel around the collar, where the roots and stems meet, protects phormiums from rotting in wet winters

Propagation: Remove suckers in late spring from established plants. Clumps can be divided, and the offsets replanted – they will make new plants, though they are slow to recover

139

PALMS AND PALMLIKE PLANTS

NAME: *CHAMAEROPS HUMILIS* (EUROPEAN OR MEDITERRANEAN FAN PALM, DWARF FAN PALM)

Origin: W Mediterranean
Type: Frost-hardy perennial
USDA zone: Z8–9
Description: This is the only native Mediterranean palm. It is slow-growing with stiff fan-shaped leaves that measure 2–3ft (61–91cm) across, and clumping trunks. It is a shapely, bushy evergreen, creating an exotic multi-headed specimen subject
Height and spread: 6–10ft (1.8–3m) x 3–6ft (91cm–1.8m)
Where and how to grow: It likes a well-drained and fairly fertile soil in sun, though it will also tolerate poor soil and shade.

It is slow from seed, so I would suggest you buy in a plant
Maintenance: Feed and water in the growing season for maximum growth
Propagation: In late spring remove suckers from established plants
Tip: These are much hardier than suggested, up to 14F (–10°C). However, they can also be planted in large containers in loam-based compost like John Innes Number 3 and kept in the house or conservatory for the winter

NAME: *TRACHYCARPUS FORTUNEI* (CHINESE WINDMILL PALM, CHUSAN PALM)

Origin: Asia
Type: Frost-hardy perennial
USDA zone: Z7
Description: This unique species has stiff, fanlike leaves and a slim, solitary trunk. The plants are attractive at all stages. They make pretty shrubs when small with their regular

ABOVE **Tough, shrubby *Chamaerops humilis*, the native European palm, is an essential exotic for the Mediterranean garden**

ABOVE *Trachycarpus fortunei* is a taller-growing palm, which is shapely and elegant at every stage in its development

circle of leaves, and, as this good-looking habit remains with them, they make very covetable subjects for many years while they develop in height. They are particularly cold-tolerant. A wonderful hardy architectural subject for the garden or a good container plant to overwinter in the conservatory

Height and spread: 70ft (21.3m) x 8ft (2.4m) eventually, though it is slow-growing; therefore you are realistically looking at a height of 15ft (4.5m) in a temperate garden after approximately ten years

Where and how to grow: Slow from seed so it is advisable to buy in a plant. Grow in well-drained soil in sun or dappled shade. Choose a sheltered spot as wind can damage the leaves

Maintenance: Feed and water in the growing season for maximum growth

Propagation: Can be grown from seed – but this is very slow!

NAME: *CORDYLINE AUSTRALIS* (TORQUAY PALM OR CABBAGE PALM)

Origin: Australasia
Type: Half-hardy perennial
USDA zone: Z8–9
Description: This is a relatively quick-growing, tolerant, evergreen palmlike tree, with green leaves and panicles of small white flowers in the summer. It makes an attractive, small tree for many years. Sparrows love the seed heads
Height and spread: 10–12ft (3–3.6m) x 3–8ft (91cm–2.4m) in a temperate garden
Popular species and varieties:
Cultivars of *C. australis* are much less hardy than the species. They make good container subjects; in the ground be prepared for winter loss of top growth, though they will regenerate from the base, becoming multi-stemmed clumps
C. 'Pink Stripe' This is a very colourful cultivar, with dazzling striped leaves

141

ABOVE *Cordyline australis*, growing here at the Tresco Abbey Gardens, Isles of Scilly, is a rapidly growing palm 'lookalike'

C. 'Purple Tower' An exciting purple-brown variety, which makes a good contrast

Where and how to grow: Use a fertile and well-drained soil in sun or partial shade. Can be grown from seed – but this is very slow

Maintenance: Old leaves will persist if they are not removed, making for a shaggy and untidy tree, so from late spring to late summer strip off old leaves with a sharp downward tug to reveal the trunk

Propagation: In spring you can remove well-rooted offsets. Our trees seed readily and self-set

Tips: In the ground, be prepared for winter loss of top growth, though they will regenerate from the base, becoming multi-stemmed clumps. In severe weather they can be cut down – but they will regenerate from the base

HERBS AND OTHER AROMATICS

NAME: LAVANDULA SPECIES (LAVENDER)

Origin: Canary Islands, Mediterranean, N E Africa to S W Asia and India
Type: Fully hardy to half-hardy perennials
USDA zone: Z5–9
Description: There are many species and cultivars to choose from, all intensely aromatic and very bee-friendly, with colours ranging from white, through lilac and purple, to red. They can also be used as small hedge
Height and spread: 12in–3ft (30cm–91cm) x 24in–4ft (61cm–1.2m)

ABOVE *Lavandula stoechas* subsp. *pedunculata* is a striking French lavender with its unusually long top bracts

ABOVE **Left to right front: *Rosmarinus officinalis* and *Rosmarinus officinalis* 'Albus', with Lavandula species, back right**

Popular species and varieties:
L. angustifolia*** Has narrow grey leaves.
During the middle or late summer they produce
unbranched long stalks with dense spikes of
strongly scented pale to deep-purple flowers.
Height 3ft (91cm), spread 4ft (1.2m). Z5
L. angustifolia 'Nana Alba'*** This is a
compact cultivar with white flowers. 12in
(30cm) height and spread. Z5
L. stoechas*** (French Lavender) Pretty
lavender with narrow grey-green leaves, short
stalks, and spikes of aromatic, deep-purple
flowers with bracts on top during late spring to
summer. 24in (61cm) height and spread. Z7–8
L. stoechas 'Marshwood'*** (borderline)
Striking lavender with long, bright-purple top
bracts. Reaches 32in (81cm) height, 24in
(61cm) spread. Z7–8
Where and how to grow: Grow from seed in
the spring. They like a fairly fertile, well-drained
soil in a sunny position

Maintenance: After flowering, cut the shoots
that have flowered back to within 1in (2.5cm)
of the older growth
Propagation: Take semi-ripe cuttings in summer

**NAME: *ROSMARINUS OFFICINALIS*
(ROSEMARY)**

Origin: Mediterranean
Type: Frost-hardy perennial
USDA zone: Typically Z6–7
Description: Upright, aromatic, evergreen
shrub with needle-like, thick-skinned, dark-green
leaves and double-lipped tubular blue or white
flowers from mid-spring to summer; sometimes
a second flush of flowers in the autumn (fall)
Height and spread: 6in–5ft x 5ft (15cm–1.5m
x 1.5m)
Popular species and varieties:
R. officinalis 'Benenden Blue' syn.
'Collingwood Ingram' Bright-blue flowers. 5ft
(1.5m) height and spread. Z6–7

143

ABOVE This display of assorted thymes at RHS Rosemoor, in Devon, south-west England gives a good idea of the choices available

R. officinalis 'Prostratus' A prostrate form, ideal for edging walls, rockeries, etc. Height 6in (15cm), spread up to 5ft (1.5m). Z6

Where and how to grow: Grow from seed in a cold frame during spring. Likes a well-drained, poor to moderately rich soil and a position in full sun

Maintenance: Trim shoots back during mid to late spring

Propagation: Take semi-ripe cuttings in summer

NAME: *THYMUS SPECIES* (THYME)

Origin: Throughout Europe
Type: Hardy perennial
USDA zone: Typically Z5–7
Description: Lots of mat-forming and spreading species and cultivars, very aromatic and attractive to bees. Foliage can be grey to green to variegated cream and white, and in summer they form a carpet of flowers in purple-pink and white

Height and spread: 10in (25cm) x 18in (46cm)
Popular species and varieties:
T. serpyllum Has purple flowers and matlike foliage with tiny leaves. Z5
T. serpyllum 'Goldstream' Has pretty golden variegation. Z5
Where and how to grow: Grow from seed in spring. Likes a neutral-to-alkaline, well-drained soil and a sunny position
Maintenance: Cut back after flowering if they are really vigorous
Propagation: Divide in spring and take semi-ripe cuttings in summer

EVERGREENS

NAME: *BUXUS SEMPERVIRENS* (COMMON BOX, BOXWOOD)

Origin: Europe, N Africa, Turkey
Type: Hardy perennial
USDA zone: Z7
Description: An evergreen shrub or small tree, with shiny, dark-green leaves that are 1¼in (3cm) long. It is excellent for both hedging and topiary
Height and spread: Both 15ft (4.5m)
Popular species and varieties:
B. sempervirens 'Suffruticosa' Slower growing than *B. sempervirens*, this is an ideal compact dwarf that is perfect for parterres, small hedges around flower beds or herb beds. Height 3ft (91cm), spread 5ft (1.5m). Z7
Where and how to grow: Give them a well-drained position in rich soil and partial shade; in full sun and dry soil the foliage can look dull

Maintenance: They are happy with severe pruning in spring, and can be cut several times in summer. (See Section 3, Topiary, pages 102–104, for more information)
Propagation: Root semi-ripe cuttings in summer

NAME: *CUPRESSUS SPECIES (CYPRESS)*

Origin: N hemisphere
Type: Fully hardy to half-hardy perennials
USDA zone: Z8
Description: Columnar and fast-growing evergreen trees that are good for hedging
Height and spread:
Popular species and varieties:
C. macrocarpa*** (Monterey cypress) Columnar fast-growing tree, excellent for hedging. Height 100ft (30m), spread 12–40ft (3.6–12.1m)
C. macrocarpa 'Wilma'*** Aromatic, fast-growing, golden-yellow conifer that will put on 8–10in (20–25cm) of growth per year. Eventual height of 30ft (9.1m) and spread of 3ft (91cm)

ABOVE **Clipped box,** *Buxus sempervirens,* **is the first choice for hedging and topiary in the formal Mediterranean garden**

ABOVE The pencil-thin cypress, *Cupressus sempervirens*, is one of the main vertical features of the Mediterranean landscape

C. sempervirens*** (The Italian or Mediterranean Cyprus) This is the classic cypress of the Mediterranean basin, forming a narrow evergreen exclamation mark in the landscape. Height 70ft (21.3m), spread 3–20ft (91cm–6.1m)
C. sempervirens 'Pyramidalis'*** A cultivar with a very narrow spread. Height 10ft (3m), spread 3ft (91cm)
Where and how to grow: They will grow in any soil with good drainage and full sun
Maintenance: Cut during late spring to early autumn (fall). Do not cut back to bare wood, as the leaves will not regenerate
Propagation: Root semi-ripe cuttings during late summer

NAME: *LAURUS NOBILIS* (BAY LAUREL, SWEET BAY, BAY)

Origin: Mediterranean
Type: Frost-hardy perennial
USDA zone: Z7
Description: Aromatic, rounded evergreen tree or large shrub with glossy dark-green 4in (10cm) long leaves that are useful in cooking
Height and spread: 40ft (12.1m) x 30ft (9.1m)
Popular species and varieties:
L. nobilis 'Aurea' Has bright golden foliage
Where and how to grow: Likes a moist and fertile soil with good drainage. Keep in a container and move under cover if your area has prolonged winter frost; otherwise grow as a specimen, hedge, or against a sunny wall. They enjoy a sheltered position in full sun or partial shade

ABOVE *Laurus nobilis*, the sweet bay, is good as a clipped standard specimen, as a hedge and as a container plant flanking a doorway

ABOVE Dramatic, dark-stemmed *Pinus nigra* subsp. *nigra* 'Helga', illustrated here, is a useful pine for a Mediterranean garden

Maintenance: Excellent for clipping; clipped topiary in pots either side of a front door is a popular look. Cut topiary twice in the summer
Propagation: Take semi-ripe cuttings in summer

NAME: *PINUS SPECIES* (PINE)

Origin: Widely distributed across the forests of the N hemisphere
Type: Fully hardy to frost-hardy perennials
USDA zone: Typically from Z4
Description: Evergreen cone-bearing trees and shrubs, with needle-like leaves in yellow-green through green to blue-grey, which are useful as specimens and also as wind breaks
Height and spread: 11–130ft (3.3–40m) x 15–30ft (5–10m)

Popular species and varieties:
P. pinea*** (Stone Pine, Umbrella Pine) Another Mediterranean staple. A conical evergreen pine, becoming domed in shape as it ages. Its juvenile foliage is greyish and retained for several years, to be replaced by glossy-green adult foliage. Height 50–70ft (15.2–21.3m), spread 20–40ft (6.1–12.1m). Z7–8
P. mugo*** (The Dwarf Mountain Pine) Better for a normal-sized garden than *P. pinea*. It is equally shapely, with leaves that are rich dark-green and a grey bark, but more compact. The cultivar *Pinus mugo* 'Mops' is nearly spherical. Height 11ft (3.3m), spread 15ft (4.5m). Z7
P. nigra subsp. *nigra* 'Helga'*** (Subspecies of the European Black Pine) This is a very

dramatic dark pine, with almost black bark and a domed habit. It has abundant, stiff, dark-green leaves. Height 100ft (30m), spread 20–25ft (6.1–7.6m). Z7

Where and how to grow: Likes a well-drained soil in a sunny position

Maintenance: Trouble-free

Propagation: Cultivars can be grafted in late winter. Species can be grown from seed but this is very slow

GREY AND SILVER FOLIAGE

NAME: ARTEMISIA CULTIVARS (MUGWORT, SAGEBRUSH, WORMWOOD)

Origin: Dry areas in the N hemisphere, S Africa and S America

Type: Frost-hardy to hardy perennials

USDA zone: Typically Z4–8

Description: Grown for their silvery or grey, aromatic and much-divided leaves rather than for their flowers. Excellent for foliage effects

Height and spread: 6–24in (15–61cm) x 12–36in (30–91cm)

Popular species and varieties:

A. 'Powis Castle'** An evergreen with very feathery silver leaves and yellow-tinged flowers in summer. Height 24in (61cm), spread 36in (91cm). From Z5

A. stelleriana 'Boughton Silver' and other cultivars*** A compact evergreen which has deeply divided leaves, providing striking silver foliage contrast, and insignificant small yellow flowers at the end of summer/early autumn (fall). Height 6in (15cm), spread 12–18in (30–46cm). From Z4

Where and how to grow: Grow from seed in spring in a well-drained rich soil in full sun

ABOVE **The divided grey foliage of artemisia cultivars is useful for contrast, like** *Artemisia stelleriana* 'Boughton Silver', **shown here**

ABOVE *Santolina chamaecyparissus*, or cotton lavender, has silver foliage and these pretty yellow 'button-headed' flowers

Maintenance: Cut them back hard in spring to ensure that they remain compact
Propagation: Divide in spring, root greenwood cuttings in summer
Tip: Keep cuttings of A. 'Powis Castle'** under glass in case you lose your plants during a severe winter

NAME: *SANTOLINA CHAMAECYPARISSUS* (COTTON LAVENDER)

Origin: Mediterranean
Type: Frost-hardy perennial
USDA zone: Z7
Description: This is a compact, hardy, rounded evergreen plant with lovely feathery silver foliage and bright-yellow, button-like flowers during the summer
Height and spread: 6–24in (15–61cm) x 8in–3ft (20–91cm)
Popular species and varieties:
S. chamaecyparissus 'Lemon Queen' A compact cultivar with pale yellow flower heads. 24in (61cm) height and spread
S. chamecyparissus 'Weston' A dwarf cultivar, with foliage which is intensely silver. Height 6in (15cm), spread 8in (20cm)

Where and how to grow: Likes light, well-drained soil and a position in full sun
Maintenance: Prune hard in the spring to maintain compact growth. Keep some cuttings under winter protection in colder areas in case there are winter losses.
Propagation: Take semi-ripe cuttings in summer

NAME: *SENECIO CINERARIA* (CINERARIA OR DUSTY MILLER)

Origin: Mediterranean
Type: Frost-hardy perennial, usually grown as an annual
USDA zone: Z8
Description: This plant has attractive, feltlike, silvery, much-divided leaves and loose yellow flowers. It will flower in the second year if not treated as an annual
Height and spread: Both 24in (61cm)
Popular species and varieties:
There are lots of pretty dwarf cultivars with a range of foliage, including:
S. cineraria 'Silver Dust' Very deeply divided lacy-looking leaves which are almost white. 12in (30cm) height and spread

ABOVE *Senecio greyii* 'Sunshine', also known as *Brachyglottis* Dunedin hybrid 'Sunshine', is another useful foliage plant

Where and how to grow: Grow from seed during spring in a well-drained and fairly fertile soil. Likes a position in full sun
Maintenance: Deadhead regularly
Propagation: Take semi-ripe cuttings in mid or late summer

HARDY LOOKALIKES AND MUST-HAVES

NAME: *AUCUBA JAPONICA* (SPOTTED LAUREL)

Origin: Japan
Type: Hardy perennial
USDA zone: Z6–7
Description: This is an evergreen shrub with glossy leaves and a rounded form. It has 8in (20cm) long leaves and is a useful, architectural specimen shrub
Height and spread: Both 10ft (3m)

ABOVE Shapely *Aucuba japonica*, the spotted laurel, is hardy and easy to grow with attractive variegated evergreen foliage

Popular species and varieties:
A. japonica 'Crotonifolia' This is a female plant, so it will produce bright red autumn (fall) berries. It has attractive, profusely speckled yellow leaves
A. japonica 'Golden King' This has very gold, mottled leaves that are wider than the species
Where and how to grow: They are very tolerant and will grow in all conditions, apart form a totally waterlogged soil
Maintenance: They can be pruned hard to size in spring in smaller spaces
Propagation: Root semi-ripe cuttings in summer

NAME: *FATSIA JAPONICA*

Origin: Japan
Type: Frost-hardy perennial
USDA zone: Z7
Description: This evergreen shrub has thick stems and handlike, large, dark-green leaves. It is one of the most tolerant architectural shrubs
Height and spread: Both 5–12ft (1.5–3.6m)
Popular species and varieties:
F. japonica 'Aurea' Slow-growing with gold-variegated dark-green leaves
F. japonica 'Marginata' This has grey-green leaves, which are deeply divided, and white margins
F. japonica 'Variegata' This has large, deeply divided leaves, like expressive hands, that are edged with cream
Where and how to grow: Grow in a well-drained soil. It likes a position in full sun or dappled shade. Ensure that it has protection from the wind
Maintenance: Prune selectively to keep an attractive shape
Propagation: Take greenwood cuttings during the spring
Tip: We have found that they are much hardier than is often suggested. Ours have had little difficulty in temperatures down to at least 14°F (−10°C)

ABOVE Tough and architectural *Fatsia japonica* 'Variegata', illustrated here, has glossy green leaves splashed with cream

ORNAMENTAL GRASSES

NAME: *ARUNDO DONAX* (THE GIANT REED)

Origin: Mediterranean

Type: Hardy perennial borderline, down to 10°F (–12°C)

USDA zone: Z7

Description: This is a hardy and fast-growing clumping grass, and as such it is a good, cheap substitute for bamboo

Height and spread: 15ft (4.5m) x 5ft (1.5m) and upwards

Popular species and varieties:

A. donax 'Variegata' White-striped variegation

Where and how to grow: It will grow anywhere but flourishes best in full sun with protection from wind. Prefers damp soil

Maintenance: Cut down to the base annually for best foliage

Propagation: Divide during mid-spring through to early summer

ABOVE The giant Mediterranean reeds *Arundo donax* and two-tone *A. donax* 'Variegata' are both fast-growing specimen plants

151

ABOVE *Miscanthus sinensis* 'Cosmopolitan' is one of the tallest-growing and most attractive grasses, with striking variegated leaves

NAME: MISCANTHUS SINENSIS

Origin: S E Asia
Type: Hardy perennial
USDA zone: From Z5
Description: This is a deciduous, clumping grass with arching leaves up to 4ft (1.2m) long, and 16in (41cm) long panicles of pale grey or purple-brown produced in the autumn
Height and spread: 5–12ft (1.5–3.6m) x 2–4ft (61cm–1.2m)
Popular species and varieties:
M. sinensis 'Cosmopolitan' cultivars (Silver Grass)

This is one of the most striking of the variegated miscanthus, with variegated white and bright-green foliage. Height to 8ft (2.4m), spread to 4ft (1.2m). Z7
M. sinensis 'Zebrinus' (Zebra Grass) The distinctive hardy zebra grass, with tall-growing architectural stems, has green leaves with an unusual, attractive yellow horizontal banding. Height 5ft (1.5m), spread 2ft (61cm). Z5
Where and how to grow: Prefers moist and well-drained soil in full sun but will tolerate most conditions

152

Maintenance: Dead stems can be left over winter for architectural impact but should be cut down in spring

Propagation: Divide in spring; the divisions can be slow to get going

NAME: *STIPA SPECIES*

Origin: Temperate and warm temperate areas worldwide

Type: Fully hardy to frost-hardy perennials

USDA zone: Z7–8

Description: Stipa species have bristly or tufted evergreen grasses with leaves that are often linear and either flat or rolled inwards in narrow cylinders. They have attractive inflorescences, in narrow feathery panicles, from early summer to autumn (fall)

Height and spread: 3ft–8ft (91cm–2.4m) x 2–4ft (61cm–1.2m)

Popular species and varieties:

*S. arundinacea*** (Pheasant's Tail Grass) This has loosely tufted dark-green leaves, streaked orange-brown in summer and turning orange/brown all winter. Height 3ft (91cm), spread 4ft (1.2m). Z8

*S. gigantea*** (Giant Feather Grass, Golden Oats) One of the best specimen grasses, with its dense tufts of evergreen or mid-green semi evergreen arching foliage. Height 8ft (2.4m), spread 4ft (1.2m). Z7–8

S. tenuissima (Pony Tails)*** Erect 12in (30cm) long leaves and feathery panicles that give a billowing effect. Height 24in (61cm), spread 12in (30cm). Z7

Where and how to grow: Grow in a light to medium-light, well-drained soil in full sun

Maintenance: Cut back deciduous *S. tenuissima* in spring, and cut off the dead leaves of the evergreens in early spring

Propagation: Divide from spring through to early summer

RIGHT **Stipa tenuissima is an attractive billowing grass, so it is ideal for giving soft contrast and constant movement**

Appendix – gardens to visit

Although there isn't space for an exhaustive list of gardens, here are some fabulous gardens to visit in the UK, Mediterranean and the USA to see what can be achieved. If you are interested in garden history there is also a whole world to discover in the great European historical gardens, like the Italian Villa d'Este and the Villa Lante, for example, where you can see the origins of the Renaissance and Italian style

CANADA

The Butchart Gardens, Mailing Box 4010, Victoria, BC V8X 3X4 Street: 800 Benvenuto Ave, Brentwood Bay British Columbia, Canada
Tel: +1 250-652-5256 (Recorded Information)
Email: @butchartgardens.com
Website: www.butchartgardens.com

FRANCE

Villa Ephrussi de Rothschild, 06230 Saint-Jean-Cap-Ferrat
Tel: +33 4 93 01 33 09 Fax: +(33) 4 93 01 31 10
Email: message@villa-ephrussi.com
Website: www.villa-ephrussi.com

ITALY

Giardini Botanici, Hanbury Università degli Studi di Genova 43, C.so Montecarlo – La Mortola
18039 Ventimiglia – ITALY
Tel: +39 0184-22.98.52 Fax: (+39) 0184-22.92.20
Website: www.menton.com/gardens

SPAIN

Alhambra, Granada, Spain
Website: www.alhambra-patronato.es

Jardi Botanica Mar y Murta ('Sea and Myrtle'), Passeig Carles Faust nº 10 Apt. Correus 112 17300 Blanes (Girona) Spain
Tel/Fax: +34 972.330.826
Email: jbmarimurtra@jazzfree.com
www.jbotanicmarimurtra.org/eng

Jardin Botanico Tropical 'Pinya de Rosa', Platja de Santa Cristina, Apt. 165, 17300 Blanes
Tel: +34 972.355.290 Website: www.blanes.net

The Santa Clotilde gardens in Lloret de Mar
Jardi de Santa Clothilde, Avinguda Sta Clotilde, Lloret de Mar, Girona, Spain
Website: www.lloretguide.com/buildings.htm

UK

Bicton Park Botanical Gardens, East Budleigh, Budleigh Salterton, Devon, EX9 7BJ
Tel: +44 (0)1395 568465 Fax: +44 (0)1395 568374
Email: lister@bictongardens.co.uk
Website: www.bictongardens.co.uk

Burton Agnes Hall Gardens, Burton Agnes Hall, Burton Agnes, Driffield, East Riding of Yorkshire, YO25 0ND
Tel: +44 (0)1262 490324 Fax: +44 (0)1262 490513
Email burton.agnes@farmline.com
Website: www.burton-agnes.com

Capel Manor, Capel Manor College, Bullsmoor Lane, Enfield, Middlesex, EN1 4RQ
Tel: +44 (0)20 8366 4442 Fax: +44 (0)1992 717544
Website: www.capel.ac.uk

Cotswold Wildlife Park and Gardens, Burford, Oxfordshire, OX18 4JW
Tel: +44 (0)1993 823006
Website: www.cotswoldwildlifepark.co.uk

East Ruston Old Vicarage Garden, East Ruston, Norwich, Norfolk, NR12 9HN
Tel: +44 (0)1692 650432 Fax: +44 (0)1692 651246
Email: erovoffice@btinternet.com
Website: www.e-ruston-oldvicaragegardens.co.uk

Eden Project, Bodelva, St Austell, Cornwall, PL24 2SGE
Tel: +44 (0)1726 811911 Fax: +44 (0)1726 811912
Website www.edenproject.com

Lamorran House, Upper Castle Road, Cornwall, TR2 5BZ
Tel: +44 (0)1326 270800 Fax: +44 (0)1326 270801

Mapperton Gardens, Beaminster, Dorset, DT8 3NR
Tel: +44 (0)1308 862645 Fax: +44 (0)1308 863348
Email: office@mapperton.com
Website: www.mapperton.com

Newstead Abbey Park, Nottinghamshire, NG15 8NA
Tel: +44 (0)1623 455900 Fax: +44 (0)1623 455904
Email: sallyl@newsteadabbey.org.uk
Website: www.newsteadabbey.org.uk

Overbecks Museum & Garden, Sharpitor, Salcombe, Devon, TQ8 8LW
Tel: +44 (0)1548 842893 Fax: +44 (0)1548 845020
Email: overbecks@ntrust.org.uk
Website: www.nationaltrust.org.uk

Pine Lodge Garden and Nursery, 'Pine Lodge Gardens',
Cuddra, Holmbush, Saint Austell, Cornwall, PL25 3RQ
Tel: +44 (0)1726 73500 Fax: +44 (0)1726 77370
Email: sclemo@talk21.com
Website: www.pine-lodge.co.uk

Probus Gardens, Probus, Nr. Truro, Cornwall, TR2 4HQ
Tel: +44 (0)1726 882597 Fax: +44 (0)1726 883868
Website: www.pine-lodge.co.uk

Renishaw Hall, The Estate Office, Renishaw Hall,
Renishaw, Sheffield S21 3WB
Tel: +44 (0)1246 432310 Fax: +44 (0)1246 430760
Website:www.sitwell.co.uk

RHS (Royal Horticultural Society) Rosemoor,
Great Torrington, North Devon, EX38 8PH
Tel: +44 (0)1805 624067 Fax: +44 (0)1805 624717
Website: www.rhs.org.uk/gardens/rosemoor/index.asp

Trebah Garden, Mawnan Smith, Nr. Falmouth, Cornwall
TR11 5JZ
Tel: +44 (0)1326 250448 Fax: +44 (0)1326 250781
Email: mail@trebah-garden.co.uk
Website: www.trebah-garden.co.uk

USA

Atlanta Botanical Garden, 1345 Piedmont Avenue NE,
Atlanta, GA 30309
Tel: +1 404-876-5859 Fax +1 404-876-7472
Email info@atlantabotanicalgarden.org
Website: www.atlantabotanicalgarden.org

Blake Garden President's Residence, University of
California, 70 Rincon Road Kensington,
CA 94707 (Mailing Address: 2 Norwood Place
Kensington,
CA 94707
Tel: +1 510-524-2449
Email: norcross@berkeley.edu
Website: www-laep.ced.berkeley.edu/laep/blakegarden

Denver Botanic Gardens, 1005 York Street, Denver,
Colorado, CO 80206-3799
Information Desk +1 720-865-3500
Websites: www.denvergov.org/Botanic_Gardens,
http://www.botanicgardens.org

Missouri Botanical Garden – 4344 Shaw Boulevard,
St. Louis, MO 63110
Tel: +1 314-577-9400 or 1-800-642-8842
Website: www.mobot.org

Norfolk Botanical Garden, 6700 Azalea Garden Road,
Norfolk, Virginia 23518
Tel: +1 757-441-5830
Website: www.norfolkbotanicalgarden.org

Rancho Santa Ana Botanic Garden, Mailing Address:
1500 North College Avenue
Claremont, CA 91711-3157
Tel: +1 909-625-8767 Fax: +1 909-626-7670
Email: Ann.Joslin@cgu.edu
Website: www.cgu.edu/inst/rsa

San Francisco Botanical Garden, 9th Avenue, Lincoln Way
San Francisco, CA 94122
Tel: +1 415-564-3239 ext. 303
Website: www.strybing.org

The University of California Botanical Garden,
Mailing Address: 200 Centennial Drive
Berkeley CA 94720-5045
Tel: +1 510-643-2755 Fax: +1 510-642-5045
Email: garden@uclink4.berkeley.edu
Website: www.mip.berkeley.edu/garden

The Huntington Library, Art Collections, and Botanical
Gardens, 1151 Oxford Road San Marino, CA 91108
Tel: +1 626-405-2100
Email: webmaster@huntington.org
Website: www.huntington.org

The Ruth Bancroft Garden, P.O. Box 30845
Walnut Creek, CA 94598
Tel: +1 925-210-9663 Fax: +1 925-256-1889
Email: info@ruthbancroftgarden.org
Website: www.ruthbancroftgarden.org

The State Botanical Garden of Georgia, 2450
South Milledge Avenue, Athens, Georgia 30605
Tel: +1 706-542-1244
Website for general information: www.uga.edu/botgarden

Washington Park Arboretum, University of Washington,
Box 358010, Seattle, WA 98195-8010
Tel: +1 206-543-8800
Email: wpa@u.washington.edu
Website: http://depts.washington.edu/wpa

Glossary

Areole – of cacti, the portion of the plant from which the spines orginate

Annuals – plants that complete their whole life cycle, from germination, flowering and seeding to death, in one year

Basal rosette – leaves radiating from a central point at ground level

Biennial – plants that complete their whole life cycle, from germination, flowering and seeding to death, in two years; producing roots, stems and leaves in the first year, and flowering, seeding and dying in the second year

Borderline hardy – will survive in an average to warmer-than-average British winter, but which will be cut down by severe and prolonged frosts

Bract – a modified leaf that is produced at the base of a flower or a flower cluster. They are often large and brightly coloured

Cyme – a flat- or round-topped branched inflorescence with a flower at the end of each branch

Deciduous – plants that produce fresh leaves annually at the beginning of the growing season and lose them when the growing season ends

Die down – of a herbaceous plant, where the whole plant above soil level disappears at the end of the growing season while the plant survives underground

Division – a method of propagation where a plant is split into two or more parts, with each part having its own root sytem, and shoot(s) or dormant buds

Fertile soil – soil which is rich in available nutrition for plants, from organic sources like decayed plant or animal material

Floret – one small individual flower of many within a larger inflorescence which is a massing of flowers on a single stalk

Flower spike – an inflorescence of stalkless flowers growing on an unbranched stem

Formers – of mosaics, pieces of stiff cardboard or thin wood that contain the liquid cement mixture and its mosaic design until it sets

Frost-hardy – able to withstand temperatures down to 23°F (–5°C)

Fully hardy – a plant that can tolerate temperatures down to 5°F (–15°C)

Glochids – bristles or barbed hairs carried on areoles of cacti

Grafting – a method of propagation by which a rare, slow-growing or difficult-to-cultivate plant is removed from its own roots (thus becoming the scion) and artificially attached to a more vigorous, rooted parent plant (the stock)

Greenwood cuttings – Shoot-tip cuttings which are taken after the first spring growth, so they fall between early spring softwood cuttings and later hardwood cuttings

Half-hardy – these are plants that can only go outside after any danger of frost has passed and that come indoors for the winter before frosts are likely

Hardwood cuttings – cuttings taken at the end of the season in early autumn or early winter; they consist of mature wood

Herbaceous – plants that die down at the end of the growing season

Inflorescence – a flowering shoot which carries more than one flower

Lobes – of leaves, where the leaf is split into sections part way down its length, dividing it into usually rounded segments

Microclimate – a climate that is particular to a very small area and affected by local factors, such as the higher temperatures found in a city environment because of the combination of shelter created by buildings and extra heat resulting from the escape of energy from densely packed habitation, industry, etc.

Mulch – a layer of material added to the soil surface to protect plants, suppress weeds and retain moisture

Offsetting – a plant which produces miniature replicas of itself, usually around its base

Overwinter – of tender plants, moving plants either in containers or as rhizomes, etc., and storing them in frost-free conditions during the winter, in a conservatory, for example

Panicles – a branched flower cluster

Perennials – a plant that survives for more than two seasons, often applied to non-woody plants only, but used in this book for all longer-lasting plant types

Poor soil – soil which is low in nutrition; some plants that have originated in harsh conditions prefer this to a more fertile soil

Propagate – to produce extra plants by setting seeds, taking cuttings, grafting, etc.

Prostrate – a sprawling, low-growing habit

Racemes – unbranched flower clusters

Ray florets – small often strap-shaped outer flowers of a composite flowerhead, which is an inflorescence with a central group of very tiny flowers, called disc florets, ringed by ray florets – like an osteospermum flower

Rhizome – an underground creeping stem that functions as a storage organ and produces leaves and shoots

Rich soil – soil rich in humus, which is slowly decomposing organic material that encourages both bacterial activity and earthworms and therefore improves the soil structure. Humus can be added to the soil by digging in rotted garden compost or leaf mould to the soil

Rosette-shaped/forming (of leaves) – radiating from a central point

Semi-ripe cutting – taken in the summer when the wood is semi-mature, so it is neither the soft growth of spring nor the hardwood of autumn/winter

Softwood cuttings – taken from the plants in the spring or early summer when the growth is young and flexible and has not become stiff and woody

Spathe – a hood-shaped bract around a spike-shaped inflorescence

Stem cuttings – also known as stem-tip cuttings, these are cuttings using the soft tip taken off a non-flowering shoot between the spring and the autumn

Suckering – plants which produce extra growth from below the ground by producing shoots from the original rootstock

Temperate – the geographical areas between the subtropics and the poles, which has seasons and no extremes of temperature, with all year round rainfall

Tender – plants which may be damaged if the temperature falls below 41 degrees F/ 5 degrees C; they will need winter protection, otherwise they should be treated as annuals in temperate areas

Trailing – a plant with long stems which hang down; particularly useful for baskets, window boxes, etc.

Umbel – a flat or rounded inflorescence which has a number of flowers on individual stalks growing from a single terminal point

About the author

Since 1977 Shirley-Anne has been running Glenhirst Cactus Nursery, a retail, mail-order and Internet-based plant business, with her husband Neville. Over the past 12 years or so they have become increasingly interested in growing hardy and half-hardy cacti and succulents in the garden, along with exotic and Mediterranean plants like palms and olives. Shirley-Anne has also designed and, with Neville, planted up a number of exotic/Mediterranean-style gardens in Lincolnshire, and they have created their own garden together at the Nursery.

The couple travels around the East Midlands giving talks to gardening clubs, plant societies and other groups on 'Design with Cacti and Succulents', 'Mediterranean-style Gardening in the UK' and 'A Crash Course in Garden History', plus talks on garden tourism, including places to visit and what to look for. The talks include slides, quizzes and demonstrations, and are designed to be light-hearted and entertaining as well as informative.

They are enthusiastic photographers, travelling all over the UK and Europe photographing plants and gardens for books, magazine articles and the GardenWorld Images (formerly Harry Smith Collection) photo library. They also enjoy their work as wedding and portrait photographers in the Midlands.

Shirley-Anne has written two previous books for GMC, on growing cacti and succulents indoors and out in the garden, and numerous articles on gardening and garden tourism for magazines.

Shirley-Anne can be contacted at:
GLENHIRST CACTUS NURSERY
Station Road, Swineshead,
Boston, Lincs. PE20 3NX, UK.
Tel: +44 (0)1205 820314
Fax: +44 (0)1205 820614
E-MAIL: info@cacti4u.co.uk
WEBSITE-http: //www.cacti4u.co.uk

Index

Pages highlighted in **bold** include illustrations of plants

GMC Publications
Castle Place, 166 High Street, Lewes, East Sussex BN7 1XU, United Kingdom
Tel: 01273 488005 Fax: 01273 402866
E-mail: pubs@thegmcgroup.com
Website: www.gmcbooks.com

Contact us for a complete catalogue, or visit our website.
Orders by credit card are accepted.